Deism: A Revolution in Religion – A Revolution in You

by Bob Johnson

Published by
World Union of Deists
Post Office Box 4052
Clearwater, FL 33758

ISBN# 978-0-9896355-0-9

For Thomas Paine who brought progress through revolution, both political and religious, and who did more than any other person to bring people to Deism.

Thomas Paine, born January 29, 1737, died June 8, 1809. Thomas Paine did as much as George Washington to start and win the American Revolution and did more than any other person to make religion compatible with our God-given reason through the promotion of Deism.

Table of Contents

Acknowledgments

I'd like to thank fellow Deist Ray Fontaine for all the help he has given me and the World Union of Deists over the years and for his friendship. Without Ray's help the W.U.D. would not be reaching half as many people as we are.

Without fellow freethinker Bonnie Lange this book would not have been published. I can't thank her enough! She has worked hard for years to keep the freethought flame burning by serving as the President of the Truth Seeker Company and as the publisher of the journal *Truth Seeker.* I loved her quality of never being too busy to answer questions and to share her vast knowledge.

Jayson X, the Deputy Director of the World Union of Deists, is a former Eastern Orthodox Christian priest. Jayson is a great help and gives me peace of mind knowing that if something happens to me, the W.U.D. will be in good hands. A single parent, Jayson can't reveal his full name due to the fact that it would be putting his career at risk. This goes to show how much further society needs to progress!

I'd like to thank fellow Deist Mark Brochu for his hard work and skill in helping to design the Deist emblem that is pictured on the back cover.

Pauline Rocco has helped me for years in our joint desire to bring Deism to the world through the World Union of Deist. She is greatly appreciated!

All of our Deist contacts and subscribers to *Deistic Thought & Action!* who allow us to have the resources to operate and grow thanks to their time and subscription payments are profoundly appreciated!

I'd like to thank my wife Linda and my step-daughter Traci for their patience and help. It means more than they know!

Even though my mom was a sincere Roman Catholic, she did teach me belief and love of God and my dad, who I don't believe bought into the Catholic dogma, taught me to greatly appreciate Nature. I am grateful to both of them.

I'd also like to thank all those people over the centuries who fought and worked to guarantee complete freedom of thought, speech, the press, religion and the right to keep and bear arms. By doing so they also made it possible for Deism to exist.

About the Deist Emblem
on the back cover

The Deist emblem pictured on the back cover is not a Masonic emblem.

The words at the bottom of the pyramid, "A New Cycle of the Ages – Deism" are to point out that we are in a new cycle that will see negative unreasonable elements of the old cycle, such as fear and superstition based religious belief vanish as the natural and reasonable religion/philosophy of Deism rises.

The uncompleted pyramid represents all the work and progress made by previous generations, and the fact that it is an incomplete pyramid shows us we still have important work to do. The top and separated portion of the pyramid represents humanity's potential which we're working and striving towards.

The bright light burst represents the light of reason and the Designer of both life and reason, God.

The motto "In Nature's God We Trust" differentiates Deism from the "revealed" religions in that we trust Nature's God, we don't have faith in what men tell us of God through their "holy books" that they themselves wrote. Everything is set on a background of the stars of the night sky. It is the stars which taught humanity the errors of the "revealed" religions as well as the reality of the Designer, which point us towards Deism!

"We can know God only through His works." *Thomas Paine*

INTRODUCTION

The power of Deism can be yours! Currently Deism is one of the most overlooked sources of solutions to serious problems facing both individuals and society. Deism is the belief in God based on the application of our reason on Nature. Deists see the laws/designs found throughout the known universe, the study of which is science, and we believe those designs presuppose a Designer of Nature, or as referenced in the Declaration of Independence, Nature's God. This simple, yet powerful, reason based belief and thought process offers us unlimited potential in solving monumental problems in our individual lives as well as throughout society as a whole because of the very high value it places on our God-given reason. This is truly revolutionary, a belief in God that puts the emphasis on REASON and not on FAITH.

The importance Deism places on reason is made evident by the American Revolutionary War hero and Deist from Vermont, Ethan Allen. In his insightful book *Reason: The Only Oracle of Man*, which is an in-depth look at God, religion, reason and Deism, Allen writes, "Those who invalidate reason, ought seriously to consider, *Whether they argue against reason with or without reason; if with reason, then they establish the principle, that they are laboring to dethrone,* but if they argue without reason, (which, in order to be consistent with themselves, they must do) they are out of the reach of rational conviction, nor do they deserve a rational argument."

Another example of the importance Deism places on our God-given reason and its encouraging of the use of reason over faith is found in this thought provoking quote from the great French Deist and philosopher Voltaire: "What is faith? Is it to believe that which is evident? No. It is perfectly evident to my mind that there exists a necessary, eternal, supreme, and intelligent being. This is no matter of faith, but of reason."

Deism has a proven track record of progress. In fact, not only is Deism a product of the European Enlightenment which elevated reason far above faith, thus ushering in such intense reason and the progress it brings that it destroyed much of the religious dogma of the Dark Ages, a time when Europe was ruled by Christianity, but Deism and Deistic ideas were also embraced by some of history's most accomplished people not only Ethan Allen and Voltaire, but also Thomas Paine, Thomas Jefferson, George Washington and Albert Einstein to name just a few. Key founding fathers of the American Republic believed in Deism so much that they crafted the Declaration of Independence as a Deistic document. The Declaration refers to God four times, but only in Deistic terms such as "Nature's God" and "Providence". Never does the Declaration mention Jesus, Moses or the Bible, as a Judeo-Christian document would, of necessity, do.

Ideas in this book will demonstrate how Deism is a revolution in religion and how it can bring about a positive revolution in the lives of individuals who embrace it. Currently there are literally billions of people who are followers of the various "revealed" religions. These people are taught that faith is much more important than reason. Of course, this leaves the people who accept this teaching vulnerable to real physical danger, to deceit and to manipulation. To demonstrate the truth to this statement, just look at Jonestown where 918 people who put more value on faith than they did on reason all perished. Deism's strong reliance on reason and independent thought makes cults impossible.

Since Deism puts such a high value on reason, looking at the gift of reason as second only to the gift of life itself, people who are Deists know it is vitally important to hold firm to their reason and to apply their reason to absolutely everything. It's obvious how this practice in the personal lives of individuals and in religious matters would continue into all aspects of life, which would make for a much more balanced, happy, reasonable and progressive society and world.

In a September 28, 2008 review of the documentary film *In the Shadow of the Moon* that appeared in the *Washington Times*, Gary Arnold wrote about the Deistic beliefs of Apollo astronaut Gene Cernan and described Deism as "Space Age." Deism truly is Space Age! The "revealed" religions were all founded in the dark and ignorant past, when people believed the Earth was flat and that the sun revolved around it. The Abrahamic religions are therefore primitive, backwards, religions that reject God's gift to us of reason. In the Space Age, which we are in *now*, we need a Space Age reason based belief system grounded in reality. A belief that allows us to free ourselves from the progress retarding fear based man-made religious dogmas and superstitions of the past. A belief that spurs us on to learn all we can about this beautiful and magnificent Universe we are all a part of. *Deism is that belief.* Deism is an idea whose time has come and which has the real potential to lead us out of our ancient and destructive thinking. This will then bring about much more positive actions which in turn will create much more progress centered happy individuals, and a much better society and world!

Anthony Flew, born February 11, 1923. Dr. Flew was the leading proponent of Atheism for much of the 20th Century and into the 21st Century. However, due to his deep appreciation of the Socratic principle of following the evidence wherever it leads, Dr. Flew evolved from an Atheist into a Deist and makes it clear he is not a Christian or any other type of "revealed" religionist.

Chapter 1

GOD GAVE US REASON, NOT RELIGION!

"I do not feel obliged to believe that the same God who has endowed us with sense, reason and intellect has intended us to forgo their use." - Galileo Galilei

Contrary to the claims of divine origins made by the big three "revealed" Abrahamic religions, Judaism, Christianity and Islam, Deism openly states that God did not come down from on high to deliver Deism to humanity. All of the big three make this claim regarding themselves while denying it in regards to each other. Judaism teaches that God talked directly to Abraham and to Moses and gave them instructions as to what Judaism should be based on and how it should operate. Christianity goes one step further and says that God Himself became man in the form of Jesus and told his disciples what Christianity should teach and how Christians should live. Islam teaches that Mohammed received the contents and teachings that would become the Koran directly from the angel Gabriel who brought them directly from God.

Deism openly and completely rejects all of these claims to special divine revelation from all of the Abrahamic "revealed" religions. Deism also rejects all claims to divine revelation made by any alleged revealed religion, not just by the Abrahamic "revealed" religions. Contrary to all of the alleged revealed religions, instead of pretending to have divine origins, Deism teaches that God is the *object* of Deism, not the *founder* of Deism. Deists openly recognize that God is not the originator of Deism. Deism is a man-made belief system based on the application of our God-given reason on the laws and designs visible to us throughout the known universe. Deism is, therefore, a **natural** religion/ philosophy, not a **revealed** religion. Because God-given reason is at the core of Deism, and because the claims "revealed" religions make regarding their alleged special divine revelations require us to turn off our innate **God-given** reason in order to accept and believe these ludicrous claims, claims such as Mohamed flying up to heaven on the back of the mythical creature, the Buraq, (Sahih Bukhari, Volume 5, Book 58, Number 227); of dead people coming out of their graves when Jesus was crucified and hanging out in the cemetery for a couple of days and then walking into town (Matthew 27:52-53); of Joshua making the sun stand still so the Hebrews could have more time to slaughter their neighbors (Joshua 10:12-13); etc.; it is plainly evident that Deism is much closer to God than all of the various and competing "revealed" religions which blatantly violate our God-given reason. By valuing and embracing God's gift to us of reason, we **MUST** reject the claims made by all of the "revealed" religions to divine revelations, miracles, divine authorship and everything and anything else that they promote that will violate our **God-given** reason if we decide to accept them.

We need to remember that by rejecting these unreasonable claims made by the "revealed" religions, we are **NOT** rejecting belief in God. God is **NOT** religion. It is only through attacking our God-given reason that the clergy can make us believe the nonsense their "revealed" religions are overflowing with! As Ethan Allen wrote in his thought-provoking book, *Reason: The Only Oracle of Man*, "Such people as can be prevailed upon to believe, that their reason is depraved, may easily be led by the nose, and duped into superstition at the pleasure of those, in whom they confide, and there remain from generation to generation; for when they throw away the law of reason, the only one which God gave them to direct them in their speculations and duty, they are exposed to ignorant or insidious teachers, and also to their own irregular passions, and to the folly and enthusiasm of those about them, which nothing but reason can prevent or restrain; nor is it a rational supposition that the commonality of mankind would ever have mistrusted, that their reason was depraved, had they not been told so, and it is whispered about, that the first insinuation of it was from the Priests."

Contrary to what many clergy members may say, rejection of their unreasonable claims does not make us infidels, for as Thomas Paine wrote in *The Age of Reason*, ". . . it is necessary to the happiness of man that he be mentally faithful to himself. Infidelity does not consist in believing, or in disbelieving; it consists in professing to believe what he does not believe."

When we trace the roots of Deism we find people such as the British religious philosopher Lord Herbert of Cherbury who wrote *De Religion Gentilium* in 1645. This work examines Christianity and caused quite a stir by making such heretical claims as there being no such thing as original sin, that not all Christian revelations are true divine revelations, and the authority of the Church does not deserve our faith, among many other anti-dogmatic irreligious observations. Though Herbert brings claims to divine revelations and inspiration into question, he does not reject all such claims, nor does he reject the idea of revelations and "revealed" religion as Deism does. However, this type of independent thinking in religious matters, though not directly establishing Deism, laid the groundwork for Deism. Other Deists in this time period were Anthony Collins, John Toland and Matthew Tindal. Tindal's *Christianity As Old As The Creation* was more in tune with Thomas Paine's *The Age of Reason* and Ethan Allen's *Reason: The Only Oracle of Man* since the restraints of treating Christianity and the Bible in a completely objective manner were gone.

By the time of the 18th century, Deism was firmly established among the intellectuals of Europe and North America. Such outstanding philosophers as Descartes and Voltaire used Deistic ideas as a battering ram against what they perceived as the unreasonable claims to divine revelations and teachings of the Bible and Christianity. In America Deists such as Thomas Paine and Ethan Allen worked hard to bring Deism to the people, while Deists such as Thomas Jefferson and George Washington did much to promote Deistic principles behind the scenes, without upsetting their constituents, the majority of whom believed that by questioning Christianity they were revolting against God since they mistakenly still believed that God was the author of the Bible and Christianity.

Simple reason tells us that the claims to divine origins and revelations made by all of the various revealed religions cannot be true. At the very most, only one can be true, for they all contradict each other and in most cases even contradict themselves. As Thomas Paine wrote in the first part of *The Age of Reason* regarding the "revealed" religions, "Every national church or religion has established itself by pretending some special mission from God, communicated to certain individuals. . . . Each of those churches show certain books, which they call revelation, or the Word of God. . . . Each of those churches accuses the other of unbelief; and for my own part, I disbelieve them all." In a nutshell, one person's revelation is another person's superstition. This open rejection of the assertions of the "revealed" religions that Paine plainly states is one of only two requirements of Deism, the other being the belief in Nature's God founded on reason-based reflection upon the observable order throughout Nature.

When you think about it, the assertions of having received special divine revelations that are made by all of the "revealed" religions and which are what they are all based on, they are what they derive their authority from, forces believers to replace their trust in God with trust in their religion's founders and leaders. This is because if God really did tell or reveal something to someone, once that person shares it with someone else it becomes mere hearsay. At that point, people cannot trust God as the source of the revelation, but can only trust the person or institution that told it to them and is making the claim to divine revelation. This further separates us from God.

The Creation: The ONLY Word of God

As mentioned above, all of the "revealed" religions claim that *their* "holy" books are inspired by God, or are the Word of God while the "holy" books of the competing "revealed" religions are either complete or partial books of hearsay and superstition. Deists flatly reject all of these claims of divine authorship of "holy" books made by all of the "revealed" religions. Deists believe that any book which claims God for its author needs to be held to a very high standard. Thomas Paine addressed this issue when he wrote:

"The Calvinist, who damns children of a span long to hell to burn forever for the glory of God (and this is called Christianity), and the Universalist who preaches that all shall be saved and none shall be damned (and this also is called Christianity), boasts alike of their holy [revealed] religion and their Christian faith.

"Something more therefore is necessary than mere cry and wholesale assertion, and that something is TRUTH; and as inquiry is the road to truth, he that is opposed to inquiry is not a friend to truth. The God of truth is not the God of fable; when, therefore, any book is introduced into the world as the Word of God, and made a groundwork for religion, it ought to be scrutinized more than other books to see if it bear evidence of being what it is called. Our reverence to God demands that we do this, lest we ascribe to God what is not His, and our duty to ourselves demands it lest we take fable for fact, and rest our hope of salvation on a false foundation.

"It is not our calling a book holy that makes it so, any more than our calling a religion holy that entitles it to the name. Inquiry therefore is necessary in order to arrive at truth. But inquiry must have some principle to proceed on, some standard to judge by, superior to human authority.

"When we survey the works of creation, the revolutions of the planetary system, and the whole economy of what is called nature, which is no other than the laws the Creator has prescribed to matter, we see unerring order and universal harmony reigning throughout the whole. No one part contradicts another. The sun does not run against the moon, nor the moon against the sun, nor the planets against each other. Everything keeps its appointed time and place.[1]

---

1 Please see Chapter Six regarding what *appears* to be chaotic natural events.

"This harmony in the works of God is so obvious, that the farmer of the field, though he cannot calculate eclipses, is as sensible of it as the philosophical astronomer. He sees the God of order in every part of the visible universe.

"Here, then, is the standard to which everything must be brought that pretends to be the work or Word of God, and by this standard it must be judged, independently of anything and everything that man can say or do. His opinion is like a feather in the scale compared with the standard that God Himself has set up."

Thomas Jefferson, the author of the Declaration of Independence and true friend to Thomas Paine, wrote, "I hold (without appeal to revelation) that when we take a view of the universe, in its parts, general or particular, it is impossible for the human mind not to perceive and feel a conviction of design, consummate skill, and indefinite power in every atom of its composition. The movements of the heavenly bodies, so exactly held in their course by the balance of centrifugal and centripetal forces; the structure of the Earth itself, with its distribution of lands, waters and atmosphere; animal and vegetable bodies, examined in all their minutest particles; insects, mere atoms of life, yet as perfectly organized as man or mammoth; the mineral substances, their generation and uses, it is impossible, I say, for the human mind not to believe, that there is in all this, design, cause and effect, up to an ultimate cause, a Fabricator of all things from matter and motion, their Preserver and Regulator, while permitted to exist in their present forms, and their regeneration into new and other forms. We see, too, evident proofs of the necessity of a superintending power, to maintain the universe in its course and order."

This type of reasoning is what helped the long time leading proponent of Atheism, Antony Flew, to evolve into a Deist.

21

Dr. Flew was considered the world's leading Atheist for much of the 20th century and into the 21st century. However, Dr. Flew always embraced the Socratic principle of following the evidence wherever it leads. Dr. Flew found that the evidence leads to Deism. By following the evidence he realized that the complexity of nature cannot exist without a profound supreme intelligence behind it. In his book *There Is A God: How the World's Most Notorious Atheist Changed His Mind,* Dr. Flew points in particular to the codes in DNA. It takes great intelligence to create codes. The existence of the codes coupled with DNA's ability to interpret them and to then take action to implement the messages in the codes clearly demonstrates supreme intelligence and purpose, or, as Albert Einstein described God, "a superior reasoning power."

Being a very intelligent man, Dr. Flew knew that many "revealed" religionists, Christians in particular, would try to make it appear that he had converted to one of their "revealed" religions, instead of to simple, profoundly beautiful and honest Deism. He made it a point to state that by believing in God he was not becoming a Christian or any other type of "revealed" religionist. He said, "I'm thinking of a God very different from the God of the Christian and far and away from the God of Islam." In an interview with the Associated Press, he said he's best labeled a Deist like Thomas Jefferson, and in his book he makes it very clear that he is a Deist and not a "revealed" religionist of any type.

Deism is making inroads on the other end of the belief spectrum as well. Since the Deist Bible, the Creation, is equally and freely universally available to all, it's not surprising that it's sparking similar thought processes among billions of people that lead to a Deistic conclusion. A great example is Raymond Fontaine, Ph.D., who was a Roman Catholic priest for over twenty years. In his outstanding and thought-provoking book, *My Life With God IN and OUT of the Church*, Ray explains how, while looking at the beauty of the stars one night while a priest in Africa, he realized how the organization he was then working for, the Catholic Church, had punished Galileo for the honest and accurate conclusions he had reached while studying those same stars. Ray then realized that he had to choose between what is true and real and what is false and manmade. This led him to become an active Deist. Ray Fontaine is one of the people this book is dedicated to and who is a true Deist brother of mine.

When you stop and think about what it took for Antony Flew and Ray Fontaine to give up in order to proclaim their Deism, you begin to realize the true power of Deism! Both of these men had dedicated their lives to something that eventually their God-given reason told them was not true. Not only did they have to admit that they were wrong - something very few people allow themselves to do due largely to ego problems - but they put their careers and incomes on the line to follow what they believed was true! In Ray Fontaine's case, he had to give up his career completely and immediately lost all his income. But their love of truth and knowledge was far greater than their egos and desires to be comfortable. They are both great Deists and excellent examples to follow!

Based on natural reasoning, Deists see the Creation itself as the only possible Word of God. Deism, therefore, has no "holy" books. There is not a book written by man that can even begin to compare to the beauty and intense magnificence of the Universe. And there is not a human who ever existed who could have designed and created the Creation.

In his thought-provoking essay, *Of the Religion of Deism Compared With the Christian Religion, and the Superiority of the Former Over the Latter,* Thomas Paine makes it very clear that the Creation trumps the Bible. He writes, "Every person, of whatever religious denomination he may be, is a Deist in the first article of his Creed. Deism, from the Latin *Deus,* God, is the belief of a God, and this belief is the first article of every man's creed.

"It is on this article, universally consented to by all mankind, that the Deist builds his church, and here he rests. Whenever we step aside from this article, by mixing it with articles of human invention, we wander into a labyrinth of uncertainty and fable, and become exposed to every kind of imposition by pretenders to revelation.

"But when the divine gift of reason begins to expand itself in the mind and calls man to reflection, he then reads and contemplates God and His works, and not in the books pretending to be revelation. The creation is the Bible of the true believer in God. Everything in this vast volume inspires him with sublime ideas of the Creator. The little and paltry, and often obscene, tales of the Bible sink into wretchedness when put in comparison with this mighty work.

"The Deist needs none of those tricks and shows called miracles to confirm his faith, for what can be a greater miracle than the creation itself, and his own existence?

"There is a happiness in Deism, when rightly understood, that is not to be found in any other system of religion. All other systems have something in them that either shock our reason, or are repugnant to it, and man, if he thinks at all, must stifle his reason in order to force himself to believe them.

24

"But in Deism our reason and our belief become happily united. The wonderful structure of the universe, and everything we behold in the system of the creation, prove to us, far better than books can do, the existence of a God, and at the same time proclaim His attributes."

The fact that Paine makes clear, that Deism (the simple reason-based belief in God) is the first article of all the "revealed" religions, gives Deism tremendous potential and power to bring literally billions of people together, since this one primary belief is common to all religions, simply speaking. If people can then follow the examples of people like Antony Flew and Ray Fontaine and put their egos in check while they strip away the man-made dogmas of their "revealed" religions, the world will progress light-years towards real lasting peace and progress. The more people become aware that there is such a thing as Deism, the closer we get to realizing this very positive potential reality.

"The fanatical Atheists are like slaves who are still feeling the weight of their chains which they have thrown off after hard struggle. They are creatures who – in their grudge against traditional religion as the 'opium of the masses' – cannot hear the music of the spheres."

— Albert Einstein, August 7, 1941

Chapter 2

THE *REAL* GOOD NEWS IS THAT THE BIBLE IS *NOT* THE WORD OF GOD

"Why should men in the name of religion try to harmonize the contradictions that exist between Nature and a book?"
Robert Ingersoll

As a former Christian I know how important it is for Christians to believe that the Bible is THE Word of God. I was born into a Catholic family and was an altar boy for several years. As a Catholic I assumed the Bible was from God. The Church talked and acted like it was but didn't put a lot of emphasis on that belief.

When I went from being a Roman Catholic to a Fundamentalist/Charismatic Christian at age 18, I was required to believe that the Bible was "the Word of God" and not simply a collection of manmade books with some good ideas in them.

When I was 25 or 26, I read the first few pages of Thomas Paine's *The Age of Reason* for school. I was so upset that he went against this idea that Christianity is based on the Word of God, I physically threw the book on the floor! Thankfully, a couple of years later when I was beginning to realize that Bible promises are not valid, I read *The Age of Reason* cover to cover and became a Deist.

As I earnestly and honestly read *The Age of Reason,* I began to laugh out loud due to the beautiful profound truths that were hitting me one after the other! I soon began to thank God for the fact that the Bible is **not** the Word of God!

A Christian reader probably looks at the above sentence with shock and horror. Please give your God-given reason a chance to help you see why it is a true blessing for all of humanity that the Bible is not the word of God, which I attempt to demonstrate below.

The Bible's Ungodly Origins

Most Bible believers sincerely believe that the Bible is either the inerrant Word of God given directly to the men who wrote the Bible by God Himself, while others believe it is the "inspired Word of God," meaning that although God did not verbally dictate the contents of the Bible to the Bible writers, God did directly inspire them to write what they wrote in the Bible. As we will see, neither one is true.

Theodoret, born around C.E. 393 and died around C.E. 457, was the Christian Bishop of Cyrus and a key theologian for the early Christians. His major work is the *Ecclesiastical History of the Christian Church*. In this writing he sheds some light on the ungodly origin of what we know today as the Bible.

Theodoret's writings in his *Ecclesiastical History of the Church*, Chapter XV – *The Epistle of Constantine concerning the preparation of copies of the Holy Scriptures* reveals that the Roman Emperor Constantine, who ruled what was left of the Roman Empire from C.E. 324 to C.E. 337, in C.E. 331 ordered the Christian leader Eusebius to prepare 50 copies of the "Holy Scriptures" for his inspection and approval. For doing so, Constantine paid the Christian leaders for the 50 copies of the Christian "Holy Scriptures."

Scholars believe that the ancient Bibles *Codex Vaticnus*, *Codex Sinaiticus*, *Codex Alexandrinus* and the *Peshitta* are examples of these 50 Emperor-ordered copies of the "Holy Scriptures." God had nothing to do with placing the order or for paying for it!

Everything was going well for the Christian leaders for hundreds of years after producing their first Bible. The Christian clergy were able to keep the Bible out of the hands of their mostly illiterate flocks. Their parishioners had to trust the priests regarding what the contents of the Bible contained. The clergy were free to interpret it for everyone, as they saw fit. As usual, those who disagreed with the Church's interpretations were grotesquely tortured and murdered by the Christian clergy or by their secular government counterparts. However, things began to fall apart when the German Johannes Gutenberg invented movable type and the printing press. Within 70 years of the printing press making its first appearance, Martin Luther was openly challenging the authority of the Pope and the Church in 1521 and brought about the Protestant Reformation. Soon he was translating Bibles into German, which allowed many people to interpret the Bible for themselves, thus bypassing the clergy. Allowing people to interpret the Bible for themselves lead to the creation of the Protestant branch of Christianity which did battle against the Catholic branch of Christianity. This accounted for decade after decade of devastating violence and misery throughout Christian Europe. Fortunately, this also led to people seeing what nonsensical ramblings the Bible is full of, which, in turn, led to freethinkers who openly attacked the supposedly Holy Scribbling as being unworthy of serious study. That in turn lead to Deism!

In order to try to hold on to its authority over Christians and

Christianity, in 1545 the Catholic Church held its 19th Ecumenical Council, the Council of Trent. In addition to attacking Protestantism, at the Council of Trent the Catholic Church officially closed the Christian Canon/the Bible. The end result for the Bible is the Catholic version has seven books in the Old Testament that the Protestant version of the Bible does not have. In addition, there are differences in word choices and translation style. Consider, for example, the story of God sending two bears to kill the 42 boys who teased the prophet Elisha about his bald head in 2 Kings 2:23-24. In the Protestant version of this Bible story, it says the bears were "she bears" while the Catholic version of this Bible story says only that they were bears.

The fact that the two largest branches of Christianity can't even decide on their alleged "Holy Book" demonstrates the lack of divine inspiration in either one of them.

The Bible Depicts God as Depraved

What would you think of someone who told their eight-year-old child to kill their puppy in order for the parent to know that their child feared them? I think most sane people would condemn that person for child cruelty and would say they are of the lowest type of parent and lowest type of person. I know I would.

If we truly believe the Bible, then we must believe that God is this type of terrible parent/being. Genesis 22:1-12 claims that God told Abraham to kill his only son, Isaac. Of course, at the last minute, if we are to believe the Bible, an angel told Abraham not to kill his son. It seems, according to the "good book," God told Abraham to sacrifice his son just to see if Abraham feared God enough to actually do it. If God is all knowing He wouldn't have to test Abraham since He would already know what the outcome would be.

This fact makes God's order to Abraham to kill his son even worse, for He knew Abraham would do it but he went on with the ghastly test anyways.

One Bible story I don't remember ever being taught when I was a Christian is about the Patriarch of Judaism, Christianity and Islam, Father Abraham, being a pimp! Yet, if you open your Bible to Genesis 12:10-16, you will read that Abraham, who was married to his attractive half-sister Sarah, told her to lie to the Egyptians and tell them that she is not his wife but is only his sister. He did this out of fear that the Egyptians, if they thought he was her husband, would kill him so they could have her. Doesn't this show Abraham did not have much faith in God and that he was a coward?

Disgustingly, the story gets worse. After they lied to the Egyptians, as this Bible fable goes, Sarah ended up being taken into Pharaoh's house and pleasing the Pharaoh who, for her sake, rewarded Abraham with sheep, oxen, slaves, etc.! So by pimping his wife/half-sister to Pharaoh, Abraham was made wealthy! And what did God do about this? He punished, not Abraham, but Pharaoh, who didn't even know Sarah was Abraham's wife because he believed their lie!!!

In Genesis 17:17 we learn that Sarah is 90 years old and God tells Abraham that she will give birth to a son they should name Isaac. Then in Genesis 20:2, when Sarah is past 90 years old, Abraham pimps her again to Abimelech king of Gerar! This time God threatens to kill the innocent king, but the king counters and tells God he believed the lie he was told by Abraham that Sarah was only his sister. According to this ludicrous tale, God punishes the king by making his wife and maidservants sterile but then changes his mind after Abraham prayed to God on behalf of the king so God then reopens their wombs! As allegedly happened with his pimping adventure in Egypt, Abraham receives from Abimelech sheep, oxen, slaves and also a bonus of a thousand pieces of silver! What kind of family values do Bible stories like these teach people? I wonder if these stories are included in Bibles for children?

Another revolting Bible story that seems to be accepted by many and questioned by few is the nonsensical story of Noah and the flood. As the story goes, the people on Earth were so evil (with the exception of Noah and his family) that God decided to kill every one of them. If we employ our God-given reason when reading this horrific tale, we must ask how could infants be evil? How could infants have offended God? How could they have hurt their neighbors? And what about the unborn babies? It goes squarely against all that is right and in line with our God-given reason to believe that an unborn baby could possibly have been offensive to God or could have committed an evil act against anyone! Yet, according to the Bible, in the seventh chapter of Genesis, when Noah was 600 years old, God caused the Earth to flood and drowned every animal and every person on Earth with the exception of Noah, his family, and the animals on the ark! Can you imagine the scene when the waters subsided??? Rotting, bloated, stinking, decaying human and animal corpses would have covered much of the ground. There would be millions of dead babies and pregnant women with their dead unborn babies inside of them. How can you say you love God and then try to pin atrocities like this on Him???

Some Christians believe that the babies and unborn babies that were allegedly slaughtered by God in the Biblical horror story of the flood were stained with "original sin." Supposedly, when Eve ate the forbidden fruit that the talking snake offered her and then convinced Adam to eat it as well, all of humanity not yet born was condemned by God! This myth in and of itself paints a hideous picture of God. This cruel and immoral act of condemning babies for acts committed by others before they were even conceived flies in the face of justice and God-given reason! How would you like it if the police came to your door to arrest you for murder because, 200 years ago, an ancestor of yours had committed murder? This despicable practice of condemning people not yet born or even conceived for transgressions committed by prior generations is a consistent and allegedly God approved idea throughout the Bible. However, the manmade dogma of original sin is unique to Christianity. Without this ungodly dogma of original sin, there would be no need for Christianity; for it is this nonexistent stain from original sin that the blood of Jesus is supposed to wash away from our soul. When Ethan Allen wrote his clergyman cousin and told him he did not believe in original sin, his cousin wrote back saying that without original sin there is no need for Christianity. Allen responded that he agreed, there is no need for Christianity!

A famous Bible story that should be openly rejected by anyone who values life and loves God is the Passover story. Most people who are vaguely familiar with it believe that Pharaoh and the Egyptians were holding the Jews in slavery and that Pharaoh refused all the requests from Moses to let the Jews go. This stubbornness on Pharaoh's part forced God to kill the firstborn of the Egyptians. This version of the ancient tale makes for a somewhat nice film production but profoundly strays from the actual Biblical account.

According to Exodus 4:21, 7:3, 7:13, 9:12, 10:1, 10:20, 10:27 and 11:10, God "hardened Pharaoh's heart" so

Pharaoh would not free the Jews!!! And what was the result of Pharaoh not doing what God made impossible for him to do, freeing the Jews? According to Exodus 12:12, God killed the firstborn throughout Egypt, the firstborn of both man and of the animals! This story from the "Good Book" depicts God, and not an angel of death or some other entity, as a bloodthirsty killer of babies, puppies, kittens, ad nauseam when it attributes these words to God: "For I will pass through the land of Egypt this night, and will smite all the firstborn in the land of Egypt, both man and beast." It also depicts God as far from all-knowing when it has God telling Moses to have the Hebrews put lambs' blood on their door posts, so He'll know not to slaughter anyone in the Jewish households. Wouldn't an all-knowing God be able to know which home housed Jews and which one Egyptians without the blood on the posts?

It's interesting to keep in mind that the violently-disgusting and terrible Passover story depicted in Exodus is what the so-called "Prince of Peace" was celebrating and honoring at the Last Supper!

Not only did the ancient Hebrews who wrote the Bible make God look like a cold-hearted mass-killer; they made him look like a shortsighted simpleton. In the somewhat comical Bible tale found in Exodus 4:24-26, God jumps Moses and is going to kill him, but the quick thinking Mrs. Moses, Zipporah, grabs a sharp stone and cuts the foreskin off of her son's penis and throws the bloody prepuce at his feet! This seems to have caused God to forget all about his desire to kill Moses and He lets him go. What total ungodly nonsense! It sounds more like a comedy skit from Monty Python than something you'd expect to find in "the Word of God."

How would you like it if you heard people saying you are a

baby killer, an abortionist and a mass killer of people and animals? No one I know would be happy to have a reputation like that. The question follows, if we wouldn't like to have people believe these terrible things about us, and especially if we claim to believe in God and to love God, how can we sincerely promote a book and religions that spread these types of slanderous and libelous ideas and images about our Creator and Friend? As Thomas Paine wrote, "Is it because ye are sunk in the cruelty of superstition, or feel no interest in the honor of your Creator, that ye listen to the horrid tales of the Bible, or hear them with callous indifference? . . . It is incumbent on every man who reverences the character of the Creator, and who wishes to lessen the catalogue of artificial miseries, and remove the cause that has sown persecutions thick among mankind, to expel all ideas of revealed religion, as a dangerous heresy and an impious fraud."

Holes in the New Testament

The biggest selling point of Christianity for the individual is the reward of eternity in Heaven and being saved from an eternity of burning in Hell. However, an objective look at the New Testament demonstrates that it is not even clear on this, its biggest promise, the salvation of your soul.

John 3:16 appears to be one of the most quoted Biblical passages that Christians use to show the way to eternal salvation. John 3:16 states, "For God so loved the world, that he gave his only begotten Son, that whosoever believeth in him should not perish, but have everlasting life."

As all "holy books" from all the various "revealed" religions so often do, the Bible contradicts itself. In particular, this promise of salvation through faith in Jesus is contradicted by the Bible itself, and it contradicts itself just two

35

chapters latter in the same Gospel!

John 5:28-29 says, "Marvel not at this: for the hour is coming, in which all that are in the graves shall hear his voice, and shall come forth; they that have done good, unto the resurrection of life; and they that have done evil, unto the resurrection of damnation." Just as John 3:16 makes it clear that salvation depends on simply believing in Jesus, John 5:28-29 makes it clear that salvation depends on doing good works, not simply by believing in Jesus. If you take the Bible as the Word of God, what are you to believe your salvation rests upon, faith or doing good deeds or both? And this is just one of many Biblical contradictions on the one point of eternal salvation!

Contrary to Deism, which teaches that you should do good simply because it's the right thing to do and will help to make the world a better place, Christianity teaches you should do good because there's something in it for you. Christianity is not based on altruism or on simply loving God as Deism is; it's based on reward and punishment, the carrot and the stick.

A great example of the greed mindset of Christianity is Matthew 6:1-6, where we read that Jesus allegedly said, "Take heed that ye do not your alms before men, . . . otherwise ye have no reward of your Father which is in heaven." Alms are donations to the poor and needy. Why doesn't the Bible say that Jesus said to help the poor and others because it is the right thing to do, that you will be making their lives better? Why does Christianity promote the greedy idea of helping others because you will get a reward out of it? Can you imagine how much more progress would be made in the lives of people and in the world if people could learn to let go of the greed and do good things for others simply for the sake of doing good, no reward required? What a beautiful world that will be!

A popular misconception about Jesus is that he came to bring peace on Earth. Contrary to this misconception is Matthew 10:34, which has Jesus saying, "I came not to send peace, but a sword." In addition to this pro-violence quote is Luke 12:51, which says Jesus said, "Suppose ye that I have come to give peace on earth? I tell you, Nay, but rather division." Is division the same as peace? There are several other places in the New Testament that makes it clear Jesus was not the Prince of Peace.

So many falsehoods abound in the New Testament they would require several books to cover. However, two Bible promises that I'd like to cover now are found at Matthew 21:22 and Mark 16:18.

In Matthew 21:22, Jesus says, "And in all things, whatsoever ye shall ask in prayer, believing, ye shall receive." This is pure nonsense and can be proven to be false by anyone at anytime. Pray right now for a pink Cadillac to appear in front of your home within the next two minutes. If it doesn't appear, this Bible promise is wrong. Christian clergy cannot legitimately say that this pink Cadillac prayer is tempting God since Jesus is making the offer, and by making the pink Cadillac prayer you're only accepting the offer of Jesus and entering into a contract with him.

The other empty Bible promise (Mark 16:18) has Jesus saying that those who believe the gospel will be able to "drink any deadly thing, it shall not hurt them; they shall lay hands on the sick, and they shall recover." I don't see Pat Robertson, John Hagee or the Pope rushing to take the poison test! Also, I don't see any of these Christian leaders clearing the hospitals of the sick and dying! If Christians really did have these Biblical powers to heal the sick, the millions of sick and suffering people around the world today would be strong testament to the insanely cold Christians who possess this Biblically promised healing power but who refuse to use it! If Christians continue to claim these and other Bible promises of healing powers are really true, let the Christians clear out all of the world's hospitals of their patients, particularly the suffering children. If they don't do this, then we have proof that the Bible promises are false, and we need to pressure the Christians to remove these Bible lies of healing powers from their "Holy Book."

A further demonstration that the Bible promises of getting anything you ask for in prayer and of the ability to lay hands on the sick to heal them is blatantly and painfully false can be found in children's graves in cemeteries around America. Currently, 30 states in the United States have exemptions in their statutes that protect parents and guardians of children who die due to parents and guardians who refuse to let them be treated medically and who rely on prayer instead! The Federal government also refuses to protect innocent children from their well-meaning but superstitious parents. Sadly, every year sick and/or injured children die because their parents put more trust in ancient superstitions than they do in their God-given reason.

The fact that Deism doesn't make any of these ridiculous promises gives it and those who embrace Deism a power over Christianity and its easily proven false teachings. When the Bible promises of mansions in heaven, eternal life, etc. are honestly examined, it makes you wonder if Jesus was a con-man. What would you think of someone who made those same promises to you today?

One key *assumption* of Christianity is that Jesus existed.

The Bible provides many solid reasons to strongly doubt even the existence of Jesus. One is the conflicting Bible account of the genealogy of Jesus. Matthew 1:6-16 lists 28 generations between Jesus and David while Luke 3:21-31 lists 43 generations! At least one of these genealogies has to be wrong. This doesn't sound too convincing for believing that Jesus was even a real person, let alone the Son of God! To believe so goes directly against our God-given reason.

Another Biblical inconsistency that causes anyone who values truth to seriously doubt the Jesus story is the conflict between the Gospel of John with the Gospel of Mark. In John 19:14 we read that the death sentence for Jesus was not passed until "the sixth hour," or at noon, which means the actual crucifixion could not have taken place until sometime in the afternoon. However, in Mark 15:25 we read, "And it was the third hour, and they crucified him." The third hour is nine in the morning, not noon or the sixth hour!

To further demonstrate the mythological nature of the Jesus story, all we need to do is read Matthew 27:52-53, which claims that at the time that Jesus died on the cross, "the graves were opened; and many bodies of the saints which slept arose, and came out of the graves after his resurrection, and went into the holy city, and appeared unto many." In other words, corpses came back to life and made their ways out of their graves and hung out at the graveyard for three days, or until Jesus returned from the dead, and then they strolled into town and appeared to many people! The Bible doesn't say what happened to them after their trip into town. Did they go back into their graves? Did they fly up into heaven with Jesus? Doesn't this Bible story go strongly against your God-given reason? Don't you think that if this really did happen, the Romans, who were highly organized and meticulous and who occupied and ruled that area of the world at that time, would have made a record of it? However, just like in the case of Jesus, even of his crucifixion which the Bible claims the Romans did themselves, the Romans made absolutely no record of the zombies walking around Jerusalem! Could this be because it never really happened and because Jesus never really existed?

It's interesting to note that Thomas Jefferson, often claimed by the religious right as being a staunch Christian, was a Deist who believed that Jesus was also a Deist. In a letter to Benjamin Rush dated April 21, 1803, which is often misquoted by Christians who're trying to deceive people into believing that Jefferson was one of them, states, "I am a Christian," but leave off the rest, "in the only sense in which he" [Jesus] "wished any one to be; sincerely attached to his doctrines, in preference to all others; ascribing to himself every *human* excellence; and believing he never claimed any other."

By believing Jesus was a human and not the Son of God, Jefferson would not be considered a Christian by most definitions, and certainly not by "born-againers" and the religious right.

Jefferson goes on to say in the same letter that even though many teachings ascribed to Jesus were good, Jesus' doctrines "were defective as a whole" and that the fragments that did survive "have come to us mutilated, misstated, and often unintelligible." He finishes the letter painting a picture of Jesus as a Deist who attempted to correct the Deism of the ancient Jews for which they had him crucified.

Chapter Three

PRACTICAL BENEFITS OF DEISM

"I never understood the reason why I could not settle into Christianity as was expected of me, but now I know! The reason was reason, my own God-given reason! My reason would not let me believe the contradictory and confusing stories presented to me that were not evidenced anywhere! How clear it is now, for the first time in my life, I am finally at peace inside and it feels so good! There really is happiness, peace, and unity in Deism!"
- Jane Benton, modern-day active Deist

This chapter covers some of the real and practical benefits of Deism. This is not done for the same purpose that the "revealed" religions promote their theologies, with an eye towards greed that is based on the promotion of false promises. None of the practical benefits mentioned regarding Deism have anything to do with supernatural gifts that the "revealed" religions hold out as reasons to join and to support them. I want to cover some of the benefits of Deism to let people know what's in store for them as Deists and for society in general, as a matter of fact and not as an appeal to their fear and greed.

The first and most important reason for Deism is that it is true. There are no manmade dogmas and superstitions, no pretentions to having past or present direct verbal or written communications from God. All of these false claims made by the various and competing "revealed" religions are very easy to disprove as was shown in Chapter 2. This fact is very clearly and overwhelmingly demonstrated in Thomas Paine's *The Age of Reason, The Complete Edition* and in many other books by other Deists and freethinkers.

Deism makes none of these ridiculous false claims and empty pie-in-the-sky promises, which gives a great power to Deism and to all Deists. For all sincere and thinking "revealed" religionists know in their heart of hearts that much of what they claim to believe can be easily proven false. This is a great burden on a sincere person who loves God. It makes one feel like one has to defend God, since one mistakenly associates God with one's particular "revealed" religion and all the baggage that carries. *In Deism this burden is gone!* As a Deist one is finally free of feeling like one's playing a terrible game of whackamo, always fearing that someone will unexpectedly bring up a point or fact proving a particular part of one's theology or scripture wrong. This is because in Deism there is no scripture or "holy book," nor is there any manmade dogma whatsoever. One's belief in God is justified by the designs in Nature which presuppose the Designer of Nature! Thomas Paine was right when he wrote that "there is a happiness in Deism, when rightly understood, that is not to be found in any other system of religion." And this happiness that individual Deists enjoy in Deism is because our God-given reason is not shocked or contradicted by anything in Deism. This beautiful unity of God-given reason and belief that Deism offers everyone brings such profound peace of mind it's hard to actually describe it. *What a wonderful and fulfilling life Deism makes possible!*

Knowing that we're not Deists because we were promised a ticket to Heaven or Paradise allows another practical benefit for Deists: the realization that **we love God unconditionally**. This unconditional love on our part allows us to trust even more in God. No longer do we fear God, but instead, we look at God as our Creator and best friend ever. This is something to be very thankful for!

This keen sense of trust in and love of our Creator frees us from the fear of burning in Hell. As Deists, we think so highly of God that we no longer associate such despicable traits as burning people alive for eternity with our Creator. Our God-given reason lets us know the entire idea of eternal damnation and punishment is the product of mere men who wanted to control their fellow men with fear. To quote the great scientist Marie Curie, "Nothing in life is to be feared, it is only to be understood. Now is the time to understand more, so that we may fear less."

This no-fear approach to God is unique to Deism and is not found in any of the "revealed" religions. As Thomas Paine wrote in *The Age of Reason*, "Were man impressed as fully and as strongly as he ought to be with the belief of a God, his moral life would be regulated by the force of that belief; he would stand in awe of God and of himself, and would not do the thing that could not be concealed from either. To give this belief the full opportunity of force, it is necessary that it acts alone. This is Deism."

Just think of the real progress that people can bring into their own lives and into society with their defeat of fear. Without fear, people can at last lift the veil from the "sacred" temples and realize the temples of the "revealed" religions are all completely empty! What pure joy that realization brings! Relief and happiness explode within us when we then realize that there is no blood soaked Bible god waiting for us to fail so he can burn us in Hell forever. That there is no reason to believe that God said the Jews are "above all people that are upon the face of the earth" (Deuteronomy 7:6) and that any country that does not serve Israel shall perish (Isaiah 60:12). How happy it makes one feel when one realizes that there is absolutely no reason to believe that God is so insecure that God's name is Jealous

(Exodus 34:14), or that He wants you to stone disobedient children to death (Leviticus 20:9) or that God's character is so sick that he would say, "Behold, I will corrupt your seed, and spread dung upon your faces" (Malachi 2:3). Deism smashes these despicable Biblical images of God with God-given reason! What a great gift; What great progress!

This Deistic no-fear approach also allows us to see that God is not so stupid as to allow Himself to be backed into a corner where the only way God can possibly save humanity from eternal Hell is to get a teenage Jewish girl pregnant and then have God's only begotten Son, who is the product of His encounter with the teenage girl, beat and nailed to a cross to die. How incompetent does the Bible portray the Creator of the Universe! Accepting ideas like this about our Creator shows we have no real meaningful love or respect for God and we have no grasp of reality. Surely, the Designer of the Universe is not such a bungling fool!

One doctrine unique to Christianity is a particularly terrible hindrance to a realistically positive self-image, which is a prerequisite for self-confidence in adults but is especially important for children. This hindrance is the teaching of the Christian doctrine of original sin. According to this harmful Christian doctrine, Adam and Eve ate fruit from the tree of knowledge of good and evil that a standing upright talking snake (Genesis 3:14 has God telling the snake that as punishment for tricking Eve he will from that day forward crawl on his belly, or "upon thy belly shalt thou go". If being on his belly was a punishment that started on that day, prior to the punishment the snake must have been walking upright or at least on legs! Or maybe he was bouncing around the garden like a self-propelled pogo stick) offered to Eve in the Garden of Eden. Since, as the ancient fable goes, God had forbidden them to eat from that tree, sin en-

44

tered into the world when they disobeyed God by eating the forbidden fruit. Once sin had entered, according to the manmade Christian dogma of original sin, all people from the first people on Earth, Adam and Eve, all the way through today and including all people on Earth for all time to come are and will be stained with this original sin which prohibits them from any communion with God and which condemns them, even though they had nothing to do with it, to suffering eternally in Hell.

This Christian doctrine goes against every kind of justice and God-given reason! How can we think so little of the Creator of the Universe that we think God would be so inept as to allow something like this to happen? And how can we ever believe that God would punish people for something they didn't do? When we look at an innocent baby, can we seriously believe this beautiful child is born stained with sin? Is it a good idea to teach our children that they are born with sin and in order to remove that sin God had to produce a son and have him humiliated, whipped, tortured and crucified so their sin could be washed away? The guilt this Christian myth places on children is nothing but evil and wrong.

The motive for the repugnant idea of original sin is to give a reason for Christianity, to keep it in business and to infect people with the sickness of unearned guilt. As mentioned above in Chapter 2, without the manmade doctrine of original sin, there is absolutely no need for Christianity, thank God.

As an honest objective look at the Bible makes painfully obvious, the Bible is a terrible book for people to attempt to understand and to follow. Two ungodly tragedies that make this clear can be found in Andrea Yates and Deanna Laney.

Andrea Yates was a married, Bible-believing Christian mother of five beautiful little children. As a Christian and a Bible believer, Mrs. Yates "knew" that Satan was a reality. She also "knew" from her Bible studies that sometimes Satan takes possession of people, even of Christians. This twisted unreasonable Bible myth, coupled with Mrs. Yates' suffering from postpartum depression, caused her to really believe that she was possessed by Satan who wanted the souls of her innocent children. She decided to drown her children "before they reached the age of accountability," which, according to her Christian superstition, would make it impossible for Satan to get their souls. On June 20, 2001 Andrea Yates killed all five of her children; Noah, seven; John, five; Paul, three; Luke, two; and Mary, six months, by drowning.

In 2003 a 39-year-old mother of three, Deanna Laney, who was also suffering from belief in Christianity and the Bible, sincerely believed God told her to kill her three children. Much like the sick Bible story of God telling Abraham to kill his Son, Mrs. Laney believed God was now telling her to kill her three sons. So, on the Friday night before Mother's Day in 2003, Mrs. Laney killed her eight-year-old son Joshua and her six-year-old son Luke with large rocks weighing 3 to 14 pounds. Her third son, 14-month-old Aaron, did not die from her attack but is now severely handicapped. She told the court, "I thought I was being told by the Lord to do this. I believe that with all my heart."

If both of these women had a more realistic and natural view of God, they NEVER would believe that God would want them to do what they did! If they were Deists, they would have been free of the delusional, violent and cruel images of God that Christianity and the Bible put in their minds. As Deists, their God-given reason would have allowed them to see just what the Bible really is, nothing but ancient Semitic gibberish not worthy of serious consideration. And the innocent children would still be alive and unharmed. Rejection of our God-given reason has a terrible price!

DEATH

People fear the unknown. Charlatans know this, hence the success of the "revealed" religions. One thing that is guaranteed to all people is death. And one thing no one **knows** about is what happens, if anything, when our body dies. This has been a gold mine for the "revealed" religions. Judaism, Christianity and Islam teach that if you follow their holy books and believe in their dogmas you will go to Heaven or Paradise.

Unlike the "revealed" religions, the natural religion/belief of Deism doesn't make any such promise. Deism plainly and honestly says that nobody **knows** for certain what happens to us when we die. We don't even know for sure if there is an afterlife let alone what it's like. This honesty of Deism can't be found in the "revealed" religions.

Since there is no man-made dogma in Deism, Deists are free to believe whatever makes the most sense to them about issues like death and an afterlife. I know Deists who believe death is final and that there is no afterlife of any kind, and I know Deists who believe there is a continuation of our consciousness of existence after our body dies. Personally, I know that I don't know, but, like Thomas Paine, I don't worry about it because I trust God as my Creator and Friend and realize we should be spending our time and energy trying to make progress for ourselves and the world and not waste them worrying about something we know nothing about. This chasing after a good afterlife and neglecting the here and now is what Gibbon in his *The Decline and Fall of the Roman Empire* attributes as a key reason to the fall of Rome. Perhaps, in their anger and hatred for Gentiles, Jews such as Saul, a.k.a. Paul, used Christianity to do exactly that, to bring down the biggest enemy of Judaism at the time, Rome. It's interesting to note that in their fourth council of Carthage in 398, the Christian leadership "forbade bishops to read the books of the gentiles."[2] That virtually limited the bishops, who made up a very large bulk of the people who could actually read, to ancient Hebrew texts full of superstition, fear and Jewish supremacy and outlawed the books of real value and meaning written in Greek and Latin. This infection and eventual dominance of Semitic superstition of the Roman Empire is what brought on the Dark Ages. And if something isn't done in today's nuclear age to curtail the influence and violence of the "revealed" religions, we will face another Dark Age or irreversible total annihilation and extinction through nuclear warfare.

This focus on making a better world in the here and now, and its relegation of questions about an afterlife to the back burner, gives Deism even more importance and potential. It allows us to bring true progress on Earth right here and right now, while giving Deists comfort and contentment in knowing that whatever happens at the time of their death, even if it's nothing at all, it is part of the Designer's design.

Personally, when my mother died, this knowledge that death is another one of the Designer's designs profoundly helped me deal with her death. It doesn't mean that I don't miss her, but knowing this fact takes the sting out of losing her.

---

2 *The Renaissance of the Twelfth Century*, Charles Homer Haskins, Meridian Books, p. 95

During Thomas Paine's adventurous and exceedingly well-accomplished life, he came close to death many times. In fact, he put off writing his thoughts about God and religion in *The Age of Reason* until he strongly believed he was very close to death, because he believed he would write in the most honest way possible knowing that he was about to die. That time came when he was in France during the French Revolution. Many of his friends and associates were being arrested and having their heads cut off, and he thought he would very soon meet the same fate. He then wrote the first part of *The Age of Reason* and completed the first part only hours before being arrested. In the second part of *The Age of Reason*, which he wrote after his release from prison, Paine wrote that while he was languishing and waiting to die in the Luxembourg prison and was very close to death from both a severe illness and possible execution via the guillotine, he wrote, "I remembered with renewed satisfaction, and congratulated myself most sincerely, on having written the former part of *The Age of Reason*. I had then but little expectation of surviving, and those about me had less. I know, therefore, by experience, the conscientious trial of my own principles." This is very encouraging to all Deists!

Thomas Paine gave some great advice to his Christian friend and initiator of the American Revolution, Sam Adams, regarding dealing with death and trusting God. It is outstanding advice we can all benefit from. In a letter to Adams, Paine wrote, "You will see by my third letter to the citizens of the United States that I have been exposed to, and preserved through, many dangers; but instead of buffeting the Deity with prayers as if I distrusted Him, or must dictate to Him, I reposed myself on His protection; and you, my friend, will find, even in your last moments, more consolation in the silence of resignation than in the murmuring wish of a prayer."

DEISM HELPS DEFEAT STRESS

One principle key to Deism is simplification. It's obvious that Deism simplifies belief in God by sticking to what is rational and natural. By this process everything that is not necessary and reasonable is stripped away. Deists believe in God. All the extras (like manmade dogmas, rituals, superstitions and all other excess needless baggage) are gone.

Likewise, Deism allows us to apply this same principle of simplification to all aspects of our lives. When we look at our responsibility to God, we see it is very simple. It is to live our life in accordance with reason and Nature, which we are all a part of. Deism is very similar to Stoicism in this respect. In fact, the Roman Stoic Seneca wrote that the Stoic motto is, "Live according to Nature." The ancient Stoics understood this realization well. Epictetus wrote that, "the wise life, which leads to tranquility, comes from conforming to Nature and to Reason." One of Epictetus' students, the Roman Emperor Marcus Aurelius, wrote, "Live according to Nature the remainder of your life."

This sound Stoic advice fits perfectly with Deism. It reflects the words of Thomas Paine regarding his lack of concern with an afterlife due to his strong trust of God. This advice goes a very long way in helping us realize that much of what we stress over doesn't really even matter. Our God-given reason tells us that worrying and stressing about things is a waste of our time and energy, for by worrying we are not making things better, we're making them worse. And many times what we're stressed over never comes about. The Deist Ben Franklin summed it up best when he wrote, "If evils come not, then our fears in vain: And if they do, fear but augments the pain." Thank God for reason!

Chapter Four

ATHENS v. JERUSALEM

"Judaism is a concern with return; it is not a concern with progress. 'Return' can easily be expressed in biblical Hebrew; 'progress' cannot." — Leo Strauss

Currently there is a war going on that most people aren't even aware of, the war between Athens and Jerusalem. Perhaps one of the greatest gifts of Deism will be its ability to help reason, Athens, win out over superstition, Jerusalem. This struggle of worldviews, with Athens representing the belief in free thought and inquiry based on nature and reason as was the practice of the ancient Greeks, and Jerusalem representing blind belief based on fear in primarily the alleged revelations of the Hebrew and Christian Bibles, as well as the Koran, has been waged for centuries and is now being brought to a boiling point by the powerful neoconservative political movement which was key in bringing about the war in Iraq, and whose superstition-based mindset has made the conflicts in the Middle East unavoidable. The neoconservative mentality and goals are found in both the Republican and Democratic political parties in the United States.

Despite monumental advances in science and technology made over the last 150 years, all of which have been made by adhering to the teachings of the Athens worldview and not to the Jerusalem worldview, the Jerusalem side of this struggle is still a real threat to free thought and world progress and peace. Every day the bodies are literally piling up as the Islamic "revealed" religion of Abraham does battle with the Jewish "revealed" religion of Abraham, which is strongly backed by the Christian "revealed" religion of Abraham. While Jerusalem is largely represented by the Big Three Abrahamic "revealed" religions of Judaism, Christianity and Islam, the dominant religion in the Jerusalem camp is Judaism. Judaism is in a very practical sense supported by the neoconservative movement. Athens, sadly, is without any meaningful representation. The only ideology that has the potential to win enough popular support to actually win this crucial battle once and for all, due to its unique ability to appeal to both belief in God and to reason, is Deism.

In this vital struggle between Athens and Jerusalem, the neoconservative movement is the vanguard pushing through practical realities that hinder progress and promote superstition and violence. The founding voice of neoconservativism is Leo Strauss. Leo Strauss was a German Jewish scholar who immigrated to the US in 1937. Seeing how the Weimer Republic could not stop the National Socialists who legally gained power in 1933, he turned against secular democracy. After arriving in the US, he became a professor at the University of Chicago. All the leading neocons, from Irving Kristol and his son William Kristol, to Paul Wolfowitz, Abram Shulsky and Richard Perle, either studied under, or independently studied, the teachings of Leo Strauss. The neocon movement is definitely made up of Straussians, and Strauss is often referred to as the father of the neoconservative movement.

Believing that progress is bad because it moves beyond early superstitions and myths that were used to control the people, such as the Bible, Strauss taught an unnatural reverence for the past–specifically the Jewish past. In a speech entitled, *Progress or Return? The Contemporary Crisis in*

Western Civilization, Strauss said, "Judaism is a concern with return; it is not a concern with progress. 'Return' can easily be expressed in biblical Hebrew; 'progress' cannot." Albert Einstein summed up this ungodly mindset and Biblical attack on progress when he described watching Jews visiting the Wailing Wall in Jerusalem on February 3, 1923: "Where dull-witted clansmen of our tribe were praying aloud, their faces turned to the wall, their bodies swaying to and fro. A pathetic sight of men with a past but without a future."

Strauss thought that most people are incapable of living their lives without a belief in a God who would punish them for disobedience and reward them for obedience. In order for the people to know what this God demanded of them, Strauss, being a student himself of the Twelfth Century influential Jewish leader Rabbi Maimonides, believed the best bet was to use the Hebrew Bible. In the editor's introduction to a collection of Strauss' writings, *Jewish Philosophy and the Crisis of Modernity*, Kenneth Hart Green writes, "Strauss learned from Maimonides that religion is essential to any healthy political society, and certainly for the moral life of human beings. Over and above this, Maimonides convinced Strauss that Jewish religion, based on the Hebrew Bible, is most essential to ground a 'genuine' morality for almost every human being."

This idea of basing world society on the Hebrew Bible is damaging to all Gentiles and to all free thinking Jews for many reasons. One reason is that we can't get an honest picture of the history and accomplishments of our Gentile ancestors from the Hebrew Bible. As Thomas Paine wrote in *The Age of Reason*, "We know nothing of what the ancient Gentile world (as it was called) was before the time of the Jews, whose practice has been to calumniate and blacken the character of all other nations; and it is from the Jewish accounts that we have learned to call them heathens."

This cornerstone idea, that the Jewish religion through the Hebrew Bible should be used to control the people, is what motivates and holds together the Jewish and Christian neocons. It is the driving force that sparks increasing and unquestioned US support for Israel, no matter what the cost is to the US and to the rest of the world.

If Athens fails and Jerusalem wins this epic battle, society will be based on the Hebrew Bible. People should have full knowledge of just what that would mean.

The Hebrew Bible is a collection of writings by ancient Jews to promote themselves and the Jewish people. It's filled with absurd stories of rivers turning into blood (Exodus 7:17), unicorns (KJV Isaiah 34:7), talking donkeys (Numbers 22:28), etc. But threaded throughout this Hebrew Bible is a game plan for Jews like Leo Strauss, the Kristols, Wolfowitz, ad nauseam, to take and keep the high ground in society and in world affairs. Unlike the Christian part of the Bible, the New Testament, which focuses on the hereafter, the Old Testament is much more focused on the well being of the Jewish people and Israel in the here and now.

Start with Deuteronomy 7:6. This Bible quote has the God of the Hebrew Bible saying the Jews are "above all people that are upon the face of the earth." Getting into this mindset is a good place to start for the masses, for it stands to Biblical "reason" that to serve God's chosen people is to serve God on Earth.

This Biblical lie that the Jews are God's chosen people and are "above all people that are upon the face of the earth" is swallowed hook, line and sinker by the Christian evangelicals and fundamentalists. This is made evident by a speech Pat Robertson made to the Herzliya Conference. In that speech the televangelist said, "You must realize that the God who spoke to Moses on Mount Sinai is our God. Abraham, Isaac, and Jacob are our spiritual Patriarchs. . . . The continuation of Jewish sovereignty over the Holy Land is a further bulwark to us that the God of the Bible exists and that His Word is true.

"And we should clearly take note that evangelical Christians serve a Jew that we believe was the divine Messiah of Israel spoken of by the ancient prophets, to whom He entrusted the worldwide dissemination of His message to twelve Jewish apostles."

This Biblical idea of the Jews being selected by God as the "chosen people" turned Thomas Paine's stomach. He addressed this Biblical claim when he wrote in *The Age of Reason* about the Bible story of a king of Israel by the name of Menahem who, according to II Kings 15:16, butchered everyone in the city of Tiphsah, even ripping the unborn babies from their mothers' wombs. After mentioning this grotesque account of the Jewish war criminals, Paine wrote, "Could we permit ourselves to suppose that the Almighty would distinguish any nation of people by the name of *His chosen people*, we must suppose that people to have been an example to all the rest of the world of the purest piety and humanity, and not such a nation of ruffians and cut-throats as the ancient Jews were; a people who, corrupted by and copying after such monsters and imposters as Moses and Aaron, Joshua, Samuel and David, had distinguished themselves above all others on the face of the known earth for barbarity and wickedness.

"If we will not stubbornly shut our eyes and steel our hearts, it is impossible not to see, in spite of all that long-established superstition imposes upon the mind, that the flattering appellation of *His chosen people* is no other than a *lie* which the priests and leaders of the Jews had invented to cover the baseness of their own characters, and which Christian priests, sometimes as corrupt and often as cruel, have professed to believe."

The neocon/Straussian idea of basing society on the Hebrew Bible is working amazingly well. Of key importance in the Hebrew Bible is Israel's well-being. In Isaiah 60:10-12, we read what God allegedly said regarding Israel: "And the sons of strangers shall build up thy walls, and their kings shall minister unto thee: for in my wrath I smote thee, but in my favour have I had mercy on thee. Therefore thy gates shall be open continually; they shall not be shut day nor night; that men may bring unto thee the forces of the Gentiles, and that their kings may be brought. For the nation and kingdom that will not serve thee shall perish; yea, those nations shall be utterly wasted." If believed, this is a direct threat from God to Gentiles that if they do not serve Israel, they will be destroyed!

There is a Jewish prayer, the Shema, sometimes written Shma, which Jews are required to say twice a day, at morning and at night, which makes clear the Hebrew Bible-based neoconservative movement, or Jerusalem, wants Israel to take from their neighbors and to rule the world. During Israel's invasion of Lebanon in July of 2006 I learned about an Israeli officer in that invasion who threw himself on a grenade to save his troops. As he threw himself on the grenade, he cried out the Shema Hebrew prayer. This motivated me to learn more about this powerful prayer. What I found demonstrates that the Hebrew Bible is nothing but a plan for earthly domination by Israel.

The Shema is considered the most important Jewish prayer. When you simply superficially read about it, it actually sounds kind of nice. It promotes loving God with all of your heart and soul. This is very Deistic/reasonable. However, it also says that if you don't follow God's commandments you will suffer. Remember, the Bible god has a hair-trigger temper! And of course, this prayer is not for everyone as is obvious by its opening phrase, "Hear O *Israel*, the Lord is *our* God . . ." (Emphasis added) This prayer is taken from text in Deuteronomy 6. If you take the time to read what is above the chosen text and what is below it, you will see it is for the earthly conquest of the neighbors of Israel. In fact, the very first verse makes this clear. It reads, "Now these are the commandments, the statutes, and the judgments, which the LORD your God commanded to teach you, that ye might do them in the land whither ye go to possess it."

To paint an even worse picture of God, this Bible chapter has God telling the Hebrews that they will be able to have great things, everything from cities to wells, that they stole from their neighbors! Verses 6:10-11 disgustingly reads, "And it shall be, when the LORD thy God shall have brought thee into the land which he sware unto thy fathers, to Abraham, to Isaac, and to Jacob, to give thee great and goodly cities, which thou buildedst not, and houses full of all good things, which thou filledst not, and wells digged, which thou diggedst not, vineyards and olive trees, which thou plantedst not; when thou shalt have eaten and be full;" How disgusting is that? This is not a good motivation to say your prayers! It's a sick and twisted mindset that needs to be done away with.

The way this Bible quote makes clear that the Jews won't have to build cities or dig wells, etc., reminded me of the point Thomas Paine made about the lack of creating that possessed the ancient Jews. Thomas Paine wrote in his thought-provoking and enlightening essay "The Origins of Freemasonry" regarding Solomon's Temple, "We do not read in the history of the Jews whether in the Bible or elsewhere, that they were the inventors or the improvers of any one art or science. Even in the building of this temple, the Jews did not know how to square and frame the timber for beginning and carrying on the work, and Solomon was obliged to send to Hiram, King of Tyre (Zidon), to procure workmen; 'for thou knowest' (says Solomon to Hiram, I Kings v, 6), 'that there is not among us any that can skill to hew timber like unto the Zidonians.'

"This temple was more properly Hiram's Temple than Solomon's, and if the Masons derive anything from the building of it, they owe it to the Zidonians and not to the Jews."

This Bible chapter, Deuteronomy 6, contains a very specific reason for the Jews to "do what is right and good in the sight of the LORD" (right and good here means to say the Shema and to keep the laws and commandments the Jewish priests claim are from God) in verses 18 and 19. The reason is "that thou mayest go in and possess the good land which the LORD sware unto thy fathers . . . to cast out all thine enemies from before thee, as the LORD hath spoken." This is what the Israeli military officer who jumped on the grenade had in him mind and which he verbalized by reciting the Shema. And this proves that as long as society turns a blind eye to the violent and ignorant teachings of the Bible, Koran or any "holy" book, we will continue to remain in this deadly war-producing mode just as those in the camp of Jerusalem want. Only Deism can set us and the world free from all of this destructive superstition.

Superstitious Christians, such as Pat Robertson and John Hagee, accept the Hebrew Bible as the word of God and fit in perfectly with Jerusalem/neoconservativism. Wanting to please the Judeo-Christian god, Robertson believes the borders of Israel should be extended to borders dating back to 950 BCE! He wrote an article about this, the title of which sums up Robertson's irrational Bible-based neoconservative outlook on Israel, "The Land of Israel: A Gift From God." The borders of Israel in 950 BCE, as Robertson states, "go all the way up north to the Euphrates River which encompasses the better part of modern-day Syria. Solomon's empire went up to the Euphrates River. And Tyre and Sidon and Megiddo. And they had the Via Maris which went from Damascus all the way down to Cairo. It went as far as the area down in Gaza."

This goal of an Israel of Biblical proportions seems to be the plan of the Jewish state itself. If it wasn't, they would have returned the land they took from the Palestinians in 1967 and would be happy to let Jerusalem remain an international city instead of violating international law by claiming Jerusalem as Israel's capital and occupying the city.

The fundamentalist Christian preacher and Christian Zionist, John Hagee, believes in the Bible's Book of Revelation, which many modern Christians claim foretells the end of the world. Unlike their fellow political neoconservatives who don't usually openly speak of the religious motives for their actions and are in general very esoteric, Hagee and the Christian Zionists branch of neoconservativism are not shy about openly stating their Bible-based reasons for their actions. In the eye-opening book *Jerusalem Countdown*, Hagee pounds away at the Bible principle of Jewish supremacy and continually reiterates the importance for both individuals and world governments to unequivocally and blindly support the Jewish state of Israel. As fear and rewards are the primary weapons of the "revealed" religions and the Jerusalem worldview, Hagee makes ample use of threats from the Bible god to destroy any nation that does not serve Israel and to reward those people and nations that do Israel's bidding.

To give a case that clearly demonstrates the raw power of the neoconservatives and their brothers in the Israel lobby, all we need to do is remember what happened to Howard Dean. Dean was running to be on the Democratic ticket for president of the United States in 2000. He said the U.S. should have a balanced Middle East foreign policy. That statement makes a lot of sense. However, it means the U.S. would have to do an 180 on our current Middle East policy because our foreign policy in that region is 100 percent pro-Israel. Dean was immediately attacked, and not just by the Republicans, but by his own party, the Democrats!

Leo Strauss wrote, "According to the Bible, the beginning of wisdom is fear of the Lord; according to the Greek philosophers, the beginning of wisdom is wonder. We are thus compelled from the very beginning to make a choice, to take a stand. Where do we stand? We are confronted with the incompatible claims of Jerusalem and Athens to our allegiance." It's obvious where Deists stand and where our allegiance is, squarely with Athens and reason and against the unnatural unreasonableness of Jerusalem. Deism teaches that wonder truly is the beginning of wisdom, not fear of God who Deists see as our Creator and Friend. We have no fear of God!

If you truly believe God is a reality, then by believing things that are proven to be full of lies and myths, things that are not real such as the Bible and Koran, it is impossible to get any closer to God or to develop a realistic and meaningful idea of God. It is only through our God-given gift of reason that we can know and learn about God. That is probably the main reason the gift was given to us. A society based on the Jerusalem camp would prohibit the exercise of our God-given reason and smother it with fear and superstition, thus rendering the possibility of a true meaningful understanding and appreciation of God impossible. As Strauss' above quote makes clear, if Jerusalem wins this will certainly happen.

When we look for the source that produced the progress that exists in the world today, the progress that has done and is doing so much to ease the suffering of humanity and which can bring us the type of progress that can take us to the stars, we find it exclusively in the camp of Athens. Athens teaches us that wonder is the beginning of wisdom. How beautiful and how true that is! It is this belief that has allowed mankind to study and to understand the principles in Nature to the point of developing science, medicine, engineering and all the great and beautiful things they have led to and which have alleviated much of the suffering on Earth. When we realize that all the inventions and discoveries that make life more enjoyable, that gives us a true understanding of where we are in the universal scheme of things, and that literally save millions of lives through science and medicine, all of that has come from the camp of Athens. Because wonder is a big part of Athens and wonder leads to discovery, wisdom and progress, it stands to reason that true progress can only be found where reason is free to explore and experiment. This very fundamental quality that is essential for progress is completely absent in the Jerusalem Bible-based camp.

When science came to a screeching halt with the fall of Rome and the advent of Christianity, suffering began to run rampant. All the scientific and medical knowledge of Rome was lost to the ignorance of the Bible. God-given reason was outlawed by the Christians to the point of ripping the tongues out of people who dared to question Biblical dogma and burning them alive as they did to Giordano Bruno on February 17, 1600. This heroic martyr for Athens and God-given reason refused to pretend the Bible was correct in matters of science, when he insisted that Copernicus was right and the Bible was in error in regards to the Earth revolving around the Sun. Bruno also openly recognized that transubstantiation, the changing of the bread and wine at Communion into the actual body and blood of Jesus, is nothing but a farfetched myth and a fraud. Bruno was not the only one to suffer the pain and terror of torture and being burned alive. The Christians murdered thousands of other innocent people in the same horrific manner who dared to use their God-given reason. The last person to be murdered by the Spanish Inquisition was the Deist Cayetano Ripoll who was murdered for being a Deist and for teaching other people about Deism. He was murdered on July 26, 1826. It stands to reason that if Jerusalem triumphs over Athens, we will once again descend into the bloody and ignorant Dark Ages or worse. Will the ancient "revealed" religions stuffed with their fear and lies and which have no place in the current space age/nuclear age bring about the end of civilization through a nuclear religious war?

Chapter Five

DEFUSING ARMAGEDDON WITH DEISM!

"What has no meaning admits no explanation."
— *Thomas Jefferson on the Bible's Book of Revelation*

John Hagee and the Christian Zionists and Christian evangelicals have written thousands of books, articles and sermons praising the Bible's Book of Revelation. Even The History Channel has programs that give serious treatment to this book of ancient ramblings. The Christians claim that the book tells us of things to come, of the final battle between Jesus and Satan, Armageddon.

One of the key reasons for Christian support of Israel is, in addition to the fear the Bible put into them mentioned in Chapter 4, the belief that promoting God's chosen people in Israel will help to bring about the end times, the climactic Battle of Armageddon, after which all true believers will get their tickets punched for their trip to heaven. Since mankind now has stockpiles of nuclear weapons which can destroy life on Earth many times over, the calls for war with Iran or any other perceived enemy of the Jewish state that the charlatans are making takes on a special meaning and a very real danger for all people.

One way Deism can neutralize the deadly power that the "revealed" religions hold is to educate the world about the Bible's ungodly origins. This vital knowledge needs to spread beyond universities and permeate **all** of society. By educating people to the fact that God had nothing to do with the Bible and that it's nothing more than ancient mythology that the Roman Emperor Constantine paid for about 300 years after the death of Jesus when he ordered the Christian leaders to come up with a final canon which is today's Bible and which he hoped would help unify what was left of the Roman Empire, we take the wind out of the sails of the end timers. By making the historic facts much more commonly known, sincere people will awaken to the fact that they've been played for fools by the "revealed" religions.

One Bible book in particular, which seems to be a favorite of those who're hoping and praying for the end of the world is Revelation. Insanity, perversions of nature and violence run deep through this book from beginning to end. For example, Revelation 14:3-4 attacks the beautiful, essential and enjoyable act of making love by saying, "No man could learn that song but the hundred and forty and four thousand, which were redeemed from the earth. These are they which were not defiled with women; for they were virgins." How unnatural it is to think of sex and women as defilement! No wonder there are so many pedophiles in the Christian clergy!

Whenever I hear a preacher on the television ranting and raving about the end times and the importance of the Book of Revelation for those who want to know what is predestined by the Bible god for humanity, I always remember the words of the great Deist Thomas Jefferson. In response to a letter from General Alexander Smyth, in which he asked Jefferson for his thoughts on his, Smyth's, explanation of the Apocalypse, or Book of Revelation, Jefferson's letter dated January 17, 1825, makes very clear what Thomas Jefferson thought of the Book of Revelation. In his answer he wrote that he "considered it as merely the ravings of a maniac, no more worthy nor capable of explanation than the incoherences of our own nightly dreams. I was, therefore, well pleased to see, in your first proof sheet, that it was said to be not the production of St. John, but of Cerinthus, a century after the death of that apostle. Yet the change of the author's name does not lessen the extravagances of the composition; and come they from whomsoever they may, I cannot so far respect them as to consider them as an allegorical narrative of events, past or subsequent. There is not coherence enough in them to countenance any suite of rational ideas. You will judge, therefore, from this how impossible I think it that either your explanation, or that of any man in 'the heavens above, or on the earth beneath,' can be a correct one. What has no meaning admits no explanation; and pardon me if I say, with the candor of friendship, that I think your time too valuable, and your understanding of too high an order, to be wasted on these paralogisms. You will perceive, I hope, also, that I do not consider them as revelations of the Supreme Being, whom I would not so far blaspheme as to impute to Him a pretension of revelation, couched at the same time in terms which, He would know, were never to be understood by those to whom they were addressed."

Many people who are currently under the spell of the Christian evangelicals and the potentially Earth-destroying, deadly myth of this being the end times greatly admire America's founders, particularly Thomas Jefferson. As the World Union of Deists grows, we will continue to increase the number of people who are made aware of Jefferson's complete disdain for the Book of Revelation. As we do that, the second and third points of the above Jefferson quote will also be made clear, parts which apply not only to the Book of Revelation, but to all of the Bible and to all of the

Koran as well. These points are that it is a waste of people's time to squander it trying to figure out ancient myths and superstitions that have no rational basis. This is true of all of the "holy books" of the "revealed" religions. God (the Supreme Being) has absolutely nothing to do with these ancient nonsensical paralogisms/scriptures. Once this is accomplished, the "revealed" religions will lose their source of energy and funding, and then they will wither and die on the vine. This act will mark the beginning of true unstoppable happiness and progress on Earth for individuals and for society! Deism was born in the Enlightenment and will serve to bring true Enlightenment back to the world.

Thomas Jefferson's good friend and fellow Deist, Thomas Paine, also believed that when people spend their time trying to figure out what the Bible means, they are only wasting their time. In *The Age of Reason* Paine wrote, "The study of theology, as it stands in the Christian churches, is the study of nothing; it is founded on nothing; it rests on no principles; it proceeds by no authorities; it has no data; it can demonstrate nothing; and it admits no conclusion. Not any thing can be studied as a science, without our being in possession of the principles upon which it is founded; and as this is not the case with Christian theology, it is therefore the study of nothing."

Thomas Paine then goes on to point out that we can learn of God through Nature and science. He continues, "Instead then of studying theology, as is now done out of the Bible and Testament, the meanings of which books are always controverted and the authenticity of which is disproved, it is necessary that we refer to the Bible of the Creation. The principles we discover there are eternal and of divine origin; they are the foundation of all the science that exists in the world, and must be the foundation of theology.

"We can know God only through His works. We cannot have a conception of any one attribute but by following some principle that leads to it. We have only a confused idea of His power, if we have not the means of comprehending something of its immensity. We can have no idea of His wisdom, but by knowing the order and manner in which it acts. The principles of science lead to this knowledge; for the Creator of man is the Creator of science, and it is through that medium that man can see God, as it were, face to face."

When Jefferson's and Paine's above ideas click, it creates a happy and profound relief in people who've been suffering under a "revealed" religion. What a huge burden it is to constantly attempt to make sense out of gibberish! Once we realize we are on the wrong road with "revealed" religion, whichever one we happen to be under the spell of, our reason moves us on to the correct road, the road of Deism! And as more and more people have this experience and positive change, the further the world moves away from the self-fulfilling false and destructive prophecy of Armageddon.

Christians who buy into the Armageddon myth put great importance on Revelation 13:17-18 which reads, "And that no man might buy or sell, save he that had the mark, or the name of the beast, or the number of his name. Here is wisdom. Let him that hath understanding count the number of the beast: for it is the number of a man; and his number is Six hundred threescore and six." The number "Six hundred threescore and six" is 666. Many a Hollywood movie has been made about this dreaded 666 number! Sincere and devout Christians are willing for themselves and their families to go without food, water and shelter in order to avoid using this number of the beast. Being mislead by their ministers and priests, they don't realize that the number, in all probability, was referring to the Roman Emperor Domitian who, at the time it is believed the Book of Revelation was written, was a major enemy of the Christians and Jews.

Another fact that will help free people from the grips of Christianity and the Bible and move the time back on the Armageddon clock is the fact that 666 may not even be the number used in the original scripture! In May of 2005, Biblical scholars and scientists at Oxford University used multi-spectral imaging to examine the oldest copy of Revelation and learned that the number used is not 666 but is 616! Dr. Ellen Aitken, a professor of early Christian history at McGill University, said the scripture examined by the Oxford team predates the scripture versions that use the number 666 for the Antichrist by 100 years.

All Christian clergy should bring this important fact to the attention of their flocks. If they truly believe Satan is going to take over the world through the Antichrist and require people to put his number on them in order for them to be allowed to continue to buy and sell, in short, to live, it is imperative that the Christians know the correct number of the Antichrist! In reality, they won't, and don't, do this because it brings up the fact that the Bible is full of holes and couldn't be the Word of God. The faithful would soon start to ask, "Well, if we incorrectly believed the number of the Antichrist was 666 for all these years, what else do we incorrectly believe?" This will start the final unraveling of the entire Bible and will spell the end of many a clergyman's career!

About the only unambiguous statement made in Revelation is to be found in the first verse of the first chapter. It clearly states, "The Revelation of Jesus Christ, which God gave unto him, to shew unto his servants things which must shortly come to pass; and he sent and signified it by his angel unto his servant John." That was written about 2,000 years ago. It is evident that the things predicted in Revelation, the Battle of Armageddon and the end of the world, which "must shortly come to pass" did **NOT** happen! The more people are made aware of these Biblical inconsistencies, the more they will follow their God-given reason and leave the ancient mythology behind.

Christians also need to ask themselves why they **do** believe that an angel brought the revelation from Jesus to John but they **don't** believe the angel Gabriel brought the Koran from God to Mohammad. Neither belief is based on God-given reason, but are instead only based on the mythology that people are born into and which they were brought up to believe.

As Deism continues to grow, it will continue to put these important critical questions to the revealed religionists. Progress requires that reason takes its proper place in the spiritual and religious lives of people and society and that the natural reason-friendly religion/philosophy of Deism replace the "revealed" religions.

These two galaxies, each taking a different angle, appear to support Giordano Buno's belief that in the Universe there is no up, down, forward, backward, left or right. Bruno believed in an eternal, infinite Creator and an eternal, infinite creation.

Chapter Six

DEISM v. ATHEISM & AGNOSTICISM

"When the pretenders to atheism can produce perpetual motion, and not till then, they may expect to be credited." - *Thomas Paine*

I frequently hear from people who tell me they thought they were Atheists or Agnostics until they learned of Deism. Because of the absurdities that "revealed" religions attach to the idea of God, it's not surprising that millions of people are turned off to belief in God and therefore associate their beliefs with Atheism or Agnosticism. This is a result of confusing religion with God. Deism corrects this problem by making it as clear as is possible that God had nothing to do with the scriptures of the "revealed" religions or with the "revealed" religions themselves. They are all without exception manmade and unreasonable, and none of them has God as their author or founder even though they pretend otherwise.

Deism rejects all the beliefs of the "revealed" religions with the exception of the first belief of most religions: belief in God. This solid reasonable and unpretentious belief in God of Deism puts Deism at odds with Atheism and Agnosticism. Deists believe in God, Atheists do not and Agnostics say there is not enough evidence to allow them to decide either way. One thing that Deists, Atheists and Agnostics all have in common is that their sincere beliefs are all based on reason. They don't say they believe or disbelieve in God because of a decision based on emotion.

It strikes me as funny that Atheists admire science because science is the study of the Designer's designs. The laws and principles in Nature that science is the study of are eternal and unchangeable and are not products of man. As Thomas Paine wrote, "Man cannot make principles, he can only discover them." These principles and laws demonstrate intelligence far above our own. As a painting is evidence of an artist, so the designs science studies are evidence of the Designer of Nature.

One of the principles of Nature scientists have discovered is that the natural state of matter is rest. Isaac Newton's Law of Inertia states that an object at rest will remain at rest unless acted upon by an outside force. This book, for example, which is matter, does not move or open itself on its own accord. It takes an outside force to move it and to open it.

Motion is not a property of matter, yet we know that matter moves as in the case of the Earth which revolves and spins around the sun. Not only does the Earth move, the sun moves as does our entire Milky Way Galaxy. Thomas Paine did an outstanding job of addressing this reality of motion when he gave a speech to the Society of Theophilanthropists in Paris, France, shortly after the French Revolution. Paine said:

"In the first place, admitting matter to have properties, as we see it has, the question still remains, how came matter by those properties? To this they will answer, that matter possessed those properties eternally. This is not solution, but assertion; and to deny it is as impossible of proof as to assert it.

72

"It is then necessary to go further; and therefore I say - if there exist a circumstance that is not a property of matter, and without which the universe, or to speak in a limited degree, the solar system composed of planets and a sun, could not exist a moment, all the arguments of atheism, drawn from properties of matter, and applied to account for the universe, will be overthrown, and the existence of a superior cause, or that which man calls God, becomes discoverable, as is before said, by natural philosophy.

"I go now to show that such a circumstance exists, and what it is.

"The universe is composed of matter, and, as a system, is sustained by motion. Motion is not a property of matter, and without this motion, the solar system could not exist. Were motion a property of matter, that undiscovered and undiscoverable thing called perpetual motion would establish itself.

"It is because motion is not a property of matter, that perpetual motion is an impossibility in the hand of every being but that of the Creator of motion. When the pretenders to atheism can produce perpetual motion, and not till then, they may expect to be credited.

"The natural state of matter, as to place, is a state of rest. Motion, or change of place, is the effect of an external cause acting upon matter. As to that faculty of matter that is called gravitation, it is the influence which two or more bodies have reciprocally on each other to unite and be at rest. Everything which has hitherto been discovered, with respect to the motion of the planets in the system, relates only to the laws by which motion acts, and not to the cause of motion.

"Gravitation, so far from being the cause of motion to the planets that compose the solar system, would be the destruction of the solar system, were revolutionary motion to cease; for as the action of spinning upholds a top, the revolutionary motion upholds the planets in their orbits, and prevents them from gravitating and forming one mass with the sun. In one sense of the word, philosophy knows, and atheism says, that matter is in perpetual motion.

"But the motion here meant refers to the state of matter, and that only on the surface of the Earth. It is either decomposition, which is continually destroying the form of bodies of matter, or recomposition, which renews that matter in the same or another form, as the decomposition of animal or vegetable substances enters into the composition of other bodies.

"But the motion that upholds the solar system, is of an entirely different kind, and is not a property of matter. It operates also to an entirely different effect. It operates to perpetual preservation, and to prevent any change in the state of the system.

"Giving then to matter all the properties which philosophy knows it has, or all that atheism ascribes to it, and can prove, and even supposing matter to be eternal, it will not account for the system of the universe, or of the solar system, because it will not account for motion, and it is motion that preserves it.

"When, therefore, we discover a circumstance of such immense importance, that without it the universe could not exist, and for which neither matter, nor any nor all the properties can account, we are by necessity forced into the rational conformable belief of the existence of a cause superior to matter, and that cause man calls GOD.

"As to that which is called nature, it is no other than the laws by which motion and action of every kind, with respect to unintelligible matter, are regulated. And when we speak of looking through nature up to nature's God, we speak philosophically the same rational language as when we speak of looking through human laws up to the power that ordained them.

"God is the power of first cause, nature is the law, and matter is the subject acted upon."

Some Atheists say that Deism is using the logical fallacy of "God of the gaps" which is the practice of saying God is the reason for phenomena in science that we don't yet understand. For example, when primitive tribes or the Christian governor of the state of Georgia, George Ervin Perdue, do a rain dance and/or pray to inspire God to make it rain because they don't know enough about science to know what causes rain, they are demonstrating the God of the gaps mentality. They fill their ignorance of why it rains with the logical fallacy of the God of the gaps.

Deism is not guilty of this charge because it is very reasonable to believe that the designs in Nature require a Designer or Supreme Intelligence. As Voltaire said, it's not a matter of faith but of reason to believe "that there exists a necessary, eternal, supreme and intelligent being."

As the study of the designs in Nature, a.k.a. science, continues to make more progress, we realize that simple material mechanics is not all that is involved in life forms. As former leading proponent of Atheism, Antony Flew, wrote in his book *There is a God: How the World's Most Notorious Atheist Changed His Mind*, "The genetic message in DNA is duplicated in replication and then copied from DNA to RNA in transcription. Following this there is translation whereby the message from RNA is conveyed to the amino acids, and finally the amino acids are assembled into proteins. The cell's two fundamentally different structures of information management and chemical activity are coordinated by the universal genetic code."

Code is **known** to be a system of symbols for the communication of information and ideas. We all **know** that a code **requires intelligence,** this is just common sense. Morse code, for example, did not happen by accident. When we look at the more complex binary code that is used to write computer programs, we see it is done by sequencing the numbers 0, which represents off, and 1, which represents on. The code in DNA can be compared to the binary code but instead of 0 and 1, genetic code uses the letters A, G, C and T which represent chemicals. This very complex code exists and works in DNA. It is therefore logical and reasonable to believe that since code cannot exist without intelligence, the code in DNA was created by intelligence. The existence and workings of code in DNA, like all the laws of Nature, point us to the Supreme Intelligence. This is not a logical fallacy, it is common sense.

Atheism teaches a "negativity of the gaps." When confronted with the question of how did intelligence-dependent code get into and work in DNA, they can only lamely say it happened by accident or chance. The built-in **purpose of life**, that is to procreate, which is part of the DNA code, can't be answered by Atheism. Deists see in this purpose-driven code what Henry David Thoreau referred to as "the steady onward progress of the universe."

In George H. Smith's book *Atheism - The Case Against God*, it is stated that rationality will not lead to God. That instead, God can only be brought about by rationalization. The book describes rationality as first finding evidence, then arriving at the idea, like Newton seeing the apple fall to the ground and then discovering the law of gravity. It then describes rationalization as first accepting an idea and then searching for evidence to support it, like someone inventing the idea of God and then saying God created the universe. Deism says it is rationality and reason that leads to God. To the Deist, the evidence is the creation and the idea of what brought about the evidence is the Creator. There is absolutely nothing known to man that created itself. For example, if someone shows us a computer, and tells us that all the individual parts that make up the computer just came about by chance, that all the intricate engineering that makes it possible for the computer to work, that they all somehow just formed into a perfectly working computer system all by themselves, we would be foolish to believe that person. Reason, if we use it, won't let us believe a statement like that. Likewise, if someone tells us the ever-growing creation and its perfect order happened by pure chance, we are under no obligation to believe them. From our own experience we know everything created has a creator. Why then should the creation itself be different?

Another question posed by Atheists is, "if nothing creates itself, then who or what created God?" Deism teaches that belief in God makes much more sense than believing there is no God. However, personally I believe that God is an eternal entity of supreme intelligence. Having the quality of being eternal, God would not need a creator. As knowledge of science continues to expand, we are learning just how little we really know about the Universe. There seems to be a strong possibility through string theory, which recently made a giant step forward by accurately predicting the results of a scientific experiment, and quantum physics that time itself is not fundamental to the Universe. Of course, this has huge implications regarding the quality of being eternal.

In *Atheism - The Case Against God*, the author writes, "When I claim not to believe in a god, I mean that I do not believe in anything 'above' or 'beyond' the natural, knowable universe." Deism teaches that the Creator is knowable and discoverable through the creation itself. It is very understandable how people could be turned off by manmade religions and superstitions with their unnatural and unreasonable claims and with their bombings and financial beg-a-thons, and confuse artificial or "revealed" religion with God. However, the Atheist attitude of accepting things simply as not knowable is dangerous to the progress of humanity. Many things were not knowable in the past that are knowable today. At one time Europeans believed it was impossible to know what was on the other side of the Atlantic Ocean, but they were wrong. As we learn more about the sciences, we are learning more about the Power that put those principles in place. An eternal Being, as Thomas Paine said, "whose power is equal to His will."

Agnostic comes from two Greek words: a – means *without*, and gnosis means *knowledge*. Thus, an Agnostic is someone who believes that he or she cannot honestly know, with much certainty, if God exists or not. One of the world's greatest freethinkers, Robert Ingersoll, was an Agnostic. He wrote, "We can be as honest as we are ignorant. If we are, when asked what is beyond the horizon of the known, we must say that we do not know." His statement appears to make the assumption that God is "beyond the horizon of the known." This was incorrect in his day and it is even more so today.

We do have evidence of the Designer of Nature. Evidence is defined in the Merriam-Webster dictionary as, "a: an outward sign: indication b: something that furnishes proof." Thomas Paine offered proof above with his discussion on matter and motion just as the genetic code, which is intelligence dependent, offers strong additional proof of a Supreme Intelligence. These facts, plus the fact of design found throughout the known Universe which plainly demonstrates yet even more design such as the systematic organization of everything from galaxies to internal organs, strongly let us know there is a Designer! Albert Einstein made this very valid point when he said, "I'm not an atheist, and I don't think I can call myself a pantheist. We are in the position of a little child entering a huge library filled with books in many languages. The child knows someone must have written those books. It does not know how. It does not understand the languages in which they are written. The child dimly suspects a mysterious order in the arrangement of the books but doesn't know what it is. That, it seems to me, is the attitude of even the most intelligent human being toward God. We see the universe marvelously arranged and obeying certain laws but only dimly understand these laws. Our limited minds grasp the mysterious force that moves the constellations."[3]

WHY DO BAD THINGS HAPPEN?

The question often comes up about the suffering in the world. People wonder how God could allow it. I believe that by doing our best to take a look at the big picture we can arrive at a satisfactory answer.

Looking at the big picture, we must first realize how little it is that we actually know. As Albert Einstein said, "My reli-

---

3 *Einstein and Religion*, Max Jammer, Princeton University Press, p 48

gion consists of a humble admiration of the illimitable superior spirit who reveals himself in the slight details we are able to perceive with our frail and feeble minds." Having "frail and feeble minds," we must admit our lack of understanding and strive even harder to understand more. We also must realize that our current inability to see enough of the big picture should prohibit us from making largely uninformed judgment calls saying that God must be evil to allow so much suffering on Earth. Especially after we realize that much good usually comes out of what we see as suffering.

It's hard for people to see the big picture in most situations. For example, when I was a child I had asthma. My parents took me to the doctor on a regular basis for shots to help me overcome the asthma. I remember one time getting in the far corner in the back seat of our car trying to avoid my father who was attempting to get a hold of me to bring me in for my shot. I couldn't understand why my parents would be so mean to me as to allow a stranger to stick me with a sharp needle. I couldn't see the big picture.

Not long ago I was watching the National Geographic Channel. They showed a baby sea turtle trying to make its way to the ocean but a crab grabbed, killed and ate it. I was wondering why God would design the universe to have such suffering. Thinking about it, it dawned on me that I'm not seeing the big picture. My extremely limited view of the Creation is similar to my view of my parents when I was four or five years old being taken to the doctor for the dreaded shot. Nobody could have convinced me at that place and time that my parents were actually helping me. Of course, when I got older I understood. Maybe that's how it will be with us understanding why there is so much suffering built into nature. As we grow and learn we will see more of the big picture and then understand the purpose more. I think evolution can explain a lot of this question.

Organisms and their species evolve to make them better at survival. Based on nature, it appears more concern is placed on the progress of the species than on that of the individual. This goes directly against Christianity which places the emphasis on the individual with concepts and teachings of such things as a personal savior, of faith-healing and of individuals getting whatever they want through prayer, etc. Nature and Christianity are at two opposite ends of the spectrum! The baby sea turtle did not survive, but eventually through evolution the species of sea turtles will probably develop a better way of making it to the ocean, perhaps better camouflage or increased speed and/or awareness. If this happens, as it has been happening from the beginning of life on Earth, that will be progress for sea turtles but not for crabs. They in turn will have to develop through evolution better ways of catching sea turtles. This again will lead to yet more progress on the part of the sea turtles if they are to survive. It seems that nature is involved with never ending progress!

When we look at astronomy, we see that galaxies sometimes collide with each other. At first glance this sounds like it would be catastrophic. However, just like on the small scale of the sea turtle and the crab, when galaxies collide, it is not bad and anti-progressive. According to the Cornell University astronomy department, "collisions and mergers between galaxies are one of the main elements that drive their evolution in time. . . . There is also friction between the gas in the colliding galaxies, causing shock waves that can trigger some star formation in the galaxies." Of course, star formation leads to planet formation which leads to yet more life in this beautiful, amazing and expanding Universe!

Deism teaches that people are responsible for themselves. When we look at much of the suffering in the world today, we realize it is manmade. When people are motivated by greed, cheat each other and steal from one another, there is pain on the part of the victim that usually radiates out to others. Letting greed get the best of us is what caused the current economic catastrophe we're now suffering under. Since it is a manmade problem, God can't reasonably be blamed for it. And since it is a manmade problem, it can be corrected by man. Likewise, the terrible violence and sex crimes that innocent people, especially little children, are victims of can be eliminated if individuals would care about their fellow humans. Sex crimes and violent crimes would also be greatly reduced if society rehabilitated itself and started taking consistent actions to see to it that recidivistic criminals are kept out of society. This boils down to Elihu Palmer's statement that he made in his book on Deism, *Principles of Nature*, "Man is responsible for himself."

Deism offers the ability to increase our awareness that we are responsible for ourselves. This is because Deism does not teach we can have our sins transferred to someone else. There is no pretended "savior" in Deism who will wash us in his blood and make our bad actions and their consequences go away. What Deists do, Deists are responsible for. Likewise, if the right thing in a particular situation is to do something and a Deist doesn't take that action, then she or he is responsible for her or his own inaction. This belief and realization makes people more aware of what they are GOING to do BEFORE they do it. When enough people adopt this type of thinking, we will be well on our way to a truly progressive world with much less suffering in it.

Chapter Seven

DEISM: AMERICA'S FORGOTTEN RELIGION

"Soon after I had published the pamphlet Common Sense, in America, I saw the exceeding probability that a revolution in the system of government would be followed by a revolution in the system of religion. The adulterous connection of church and state, wherever it had taken place, whether Jewish, Christian, or Turkish, had so effectually prohibited by pains and penalties, every discussion upon established creeds, and upon first principles of religion, that until the system of government should be changed, those subjects could not be brought fairly and openly before the world; but that whenever this should be done, a revolution in the system of religion would follow. Human inventions and priestcraft would be detected; and man would return to the pure, unmixed and unadulterated belief in one God, and no more."

— Thomas Paine

Think and talk about this at least on every Fourth of July: If the Bible is correct, America's founders and everyone who took part in making the American Revolution a success are burning in Hell right now! We "know" this because the Bible tells us so!

Romans 13:1-7 clearly states that governments and government officials are from God and are to be obeyed. It states, "the powers that be are ordained of God." It continues, "Whosoever therefore resisteth the power, resisteth the ordinance of God: and they that resist shall receive to themselves damnation." It also says we should be afraid of the government. If you believe the Bible is the word of God, this Bible quote makes it very clear that to disobey government authorities brings about your damnation. Not only did Washington, Jefferson, Franklin, Paine and all people who took part in the American Revolution "resisteth" "the powers that be," they violently overthrew them!

These pro-government verses from the Bible are seen by the current government as useful tools for maintaining power. As reported on CBS's KSLA News on August 23, 2007, the U.S. Department of Homeland Security has even organized Clergy Response Teams who are trained and ready to spring into action should the American people ever decide they want to follow the Declaration of Independence and abolish the corrupt government. These Clergy Response Teams are trained to use Romans 13:1-7 to help the government diffuse any such revolutionary challenge to its existence.

Can you imagine what would have happened, or not have happened, if America's revolutionaries had actually taken the Bible seriously? If they had, the U.S. would still be a part of the British Empire! The world would probably still be existing under the fallacy of the people being ruled over by monarchies under the delusion of "divine right". Thankfully, America's revolutionaries put more importance on their God given reason than they did on Christianity or the Bible. This is reflected by American Deist Thomas Jefferson who wrote on June 24, 1826, just two weeks before his death on July 4, 1826, "May it [the Fourth of July] be to the world, what I believe it will be, (to some parts sooner, to others later, but finally to all,) the signal of arousing men to burst the chains under which monkish ignorance and superstition had persuaded them to bind themselves, and to as-

sume the blessings and security of self-government. . . .
The general spread of the light of science has already laid
open to every view the palpable truth, that the mass of
mankind has not been born with saddles on their backs, nor
a favored few booted and spurred, ready to ride them legitimately, by the grace of God."

Jefferson's Deism shines through in his reference to
"monkish ignorance and superstition" being responsible for
people being mislead to believe in the Bible-based lie
known as the divine right of monarchy. He makes it crystal
clear that God had nothing to do with the artificial aristocracy.

America's first six presidents, George Washington, John
Adams, Thomas Jefferson, James Madison, James Monroe
and John Quincy Adams were either all Deists or heavily
influenced by Deism, and none of them could really be
considered a Christian because none of them believed that
Jesus was the son of God. Prior to the American Revolution, people who aspired to political advancement and to
positions of authority that allowed them to have the power
to make positive changes in the world needed to belong to,
and be active in, the established church. This is why most
of the above listed presidents often have biographies that
list them as members of one of the various Christian sects.
But in early America, particularly in pre-revolutionary
America, you had to belong to the dominant church if you
wanted to have influence in society, as is illustrated by the
following taken from *Old Churches, Ministers and Families of Virginia*, by Bishop William Meade, I, p 191: "Even
Mr. Jefferson, and George Wythe, who did not conceal their
disbelief in Christianity, took their parts in the duties of
vestrymen, the one at Williamsburg, the other at Albemarle;
for they wished to be men of influence."

George Washington, like many of America's founders who took part in the American Revolution, was "officially" an Episcopalian. However, as the very important book *George Washington and Religion* by Paul F. Boller, Jr. makes clear, George Washington was a Deist. On page 82 of his outstanding book, Boller includes a quote from a Presbyterian minister, Arthur B. Bradford, who was an associate of Ashbel Green another Presbyterian minister who had known George Washington personally. Bradford wrote that Green "often said in my hearing, though very sorrowfully, of course, that while Washington was very deferential to religion and its ceremonies, like nearly all the founders of the Republic, he was not a Christian, but a Deist."

Many politicians today like to pander to the religious right who profit greatly from the lie that America was founded as a Christian nation. A good example is John McCain, who in an interview with beliefnet.com, openly stated that the U.S. Constitution established America as a Christian nation. The interviewer did not ask him how he can believe such a thing when the words God, Bible, Jesus or Christian are not to be found anywhere in the founding document. McCain also was not asked how the Constitution could establish the U.S. as a Christian nation without plainly saying so. I would love to know what McCain's answers would be!

Perhaps John McCain never read the Declaration of Independence or the U.S. Constitution. Maybe he only relies on the leaders of the religious right to tell him what is written in these important documents. When we read what Pat Robertson wrote on page 270 of his book *The Turning Tide,* we see it is in line with McCain's misconception. Robertson wrote, "It is certainly true that the precepts of faith are interwoven throughout the founding documents of this nation. The forms of our constitutional government - as implemented by Jefferson, Madison, Franklin, Washington, Adams, and others - were carefully designed to acknowledge the authority of the Scriptures and our dependence upon the Creator." Not only did he name five founders who were not Christians because they did not believe in the divinity of Jesus and who were Deists with the exception of Adams. If he's referring to Sam Adams who was a Christian, he's correct; but I believe he's referring to John Adams. John Adams was a Unitarian. Not only are they incorrect "that the precepts of faith are interwoven throughout the founding documents of this nation" as is more than obvious by the **complete lack** of any mention of "faith" or religion in the U.S. Constitution, with the exception of the First Amendment, which does not promote Christianity or Judaism but instead says, "Congress shall make no law respecting an establishment of religion, or prohibiting the free exercise thereof," which is the direct opposite of what Robertson is saying. Robertson's other lie about America's founders setting "the forms of our constitutional government . . . to acknowledge the authority of Scriptures" is fully exposed when we realize Article 4, Section 4 of the U.S. Constitution guarantees a republican form of government which is in direct conflict with the type of government the Bible promotes at Deuteronomy 17:15, which has God telling the Hebrews that he will decide who shall be king. In reality, of course, the priests decided who would be king, not God. To prove this point all we need to do is go up a few verses to Deuteronomy 17:12-13 where the priests wrote that God said, "And the man that will do presumptuously, and will not hearken unto the priest that standeth to minister there before the LORD thy God, or unto the judge, even that man shall die: and thou shalt put away the evil from Israel. And all the people shall hear, and fear, and do no more presumptuously." Does this sound Constitutional to you, to have priests tell the people who God wants as president or king? And to have anyone who doesn't agree with the clergy to be put to death doesn't sound very reasonable or American to me either!

This promotion of fear to control people, which the Bible is dripping with, is exactly why the neoconservatives want a society and world based on the Hebrew Bible. Fear is a great tool for the artificial aristocracy to use to control free thought and people. This is very un-American and anti-progressive! Thank God America's founders followed their own God-given reason and their own God-given consciences, and not the ungodly backwards Bible! Could you imagine living in a country where the likes of Pat Robertson or Benny Hinn would make the announcement of who God told them should be King of America or of any other country? And if you or anyone else had the common sense and courage to question these "reverends," you would be put to death!

Pat Robertson seems to be changing his tactics by disingenuously shifting from saying the Declaration of Independence and the U.S. Constitution are Christian documents to going back over 100 years prior to either of these documents, all the way back to the Pilgrims. In his book, *The Ten Offenses*, he writes, "The Supreme Court's recent interpretation of 'separation of Church and State' would have been unthinkable to our Founders in 1607 and 1620, because for them their Christian faith and their government were as one."

Yes, Pat, you are correct in that the Pilgrims did believe church and state should be united. However, these are the same people and the same thinking mired in Biblical insanity and ungodly unreasonableness which brought us the

Salem witch executions! And they are **not** the Founders of the American Republic, are they? They had absolutely nothing to do with the Declaration of Independence, the U.S. Constitution or the American Republic. In fact, their twisted thinking, falsely believing that the British monarchy was ruling over them because it was God's will, is the same type of twisted thinking of those who were alive during the American Revolution and who opposed it. They were the Tories. They did all they could to fight against America's founders and the rebel cause for independence.

ARTICLE XI.

As the government of the United States of America is not in any sense founded on the Christian religion—as it has in it self no character of enmity against the laws, religion or tranquility of Musselmen—and as the said states never have entered into any war or act of hostility against any Mahometan nation, it is declared by the parties, that no pretext arising from religious opinions shall ever produce an interruption of the harmony existing between the two countries.

One little-known document that plainly states that America was **NOT** founded on the Christian religion is the *Treaty of Peace and Friendship between the United States and the Bey and Subjects of Tripoli of Barbary.* Article 11 of this official U.S. treaty, pictured above, which was started during the administration of George Washington and was ratified during the administration of John Adams, plainly and clearly states, "As the Government of the United States of America is not, in any sense, founded on the Christian religion . . ."! Surely, even the most zealous neoconservatives and Christian evangelicals can understand what this means! Now, all they have to do is act accordingly!

Up until the American Revolution, people mistakenly believed that God ordained the monarchies to rule over society and mankind. Religion was thoroughly and inextricably mixed with government. This is what brought about such things as the Salem Witch Trials. As in Europe, pre-revolutionary America, which was just an extension of Europe, held the Bible in high esteem and seriously believed in it. It seems most people don't realize that to say you believe in the Bible means you must believe in witches and wizards and that you should kill people you think are witches and wizards! Exodus 22:18 states, "Thou shalt not suffer a witch to live." Leviticus 20:27 reads, "A man also or woman that hath a familiar spirit, or that is a wizard, shall surely be put to death: they shall stone them with stones: their blood shall be upon them."

This type of Biblical thinking caused the people of Salem, Massachusetts from June through September of 1692 to kill 20 of their neighbors, 19 by hanging and one 80-year-old man by having heavy stones placed on him until his chest, heart and lungs were crushed, because they believed they were witches and wizards! Christianity had smashed their innate God-given reason to the point of actually believing that fictional characters found in the Bible such as witches and wizards were real! If the American Revolution had not been fought and won with its ensuing principle of separation of church and state, it is very possible that today we would still be subject to this same type of deadly Biblical ignorance.

Today, politicians from both major U.S. political parties, the Democrats and the Republicans, pander to the "revealed" religions. A case in point is the "faith-based"/religious organizations that get hundreds of millions of taxpayer dollars in handouts from the politicians, thus uniting religion with government. This is clearly unconstitutional! It violates the Jeffersonian separation of church and state. One of our Deist forefathers realized this fact; and as President of the United States, he vetoed an attempt by Congress in 1811 to pass an act that would have given public money to a religious organization. James Madison, the father of the Constitution, wrote a Veto Message to Congress on February 21, 1811 explaining why he vetoed it. In his message he wrote, "Because the Bill vests in this said incorporated Church, an authority to provide for the support of the poor children of the same; and authority, which being altogether superfluous if the provision is to be the result of pious charity, would be a precedent for giving to religious Societies as such, a legal agency in carrying into effect a public and civic duty."

Forgetting about the U.S. Constitution which he swore under oath to uphold and defend, newly elected Democrat President Barack Obama is expanding former Republican President George W. Bush's White House Office of Faith-Based and Neighborhood Partnerships and is adding a new advisory board which includes members of the clergy. The Pentecostal minister who Obama appointed to lead the office, Joshua DuBois, will take advice from the board on how to spend tax-payer money on "revealed" religious organizations. This unconstitutional White House program and advisory board shows how America's reason-based

Deist roots are being smothered by "revealed" religious organizations steeped in superstition.

I'm happy to know that teachers are starting to cover the Deistic roots of America more in their classrooms. This is a very real history that is too often either not mentioned at all or is only briefly glossed over in our educational system. This is wrong. Every student should be fully aware of America's Deistic roots and the important role they played in American history. Thomas Paine's *The Age of Reason* should be read by all students in order to help them better protect themselves in all situations with God's gift to them of reason.

Chapter Eight

The Future is Deism

"I don't have a religion. I believe in God."
— Jennifer Aniston

Evolution, which is one of the Designer's designs, teaches us that the species that adapts to its changing environment is the species that survives and is therefore allowed the opportunity to continue to live, to procreate and to progress. Our environment has changed considerably from the days when the ancient Hebrews wrote the Bible. We now have, thanks to people who went directly against the dogmas of the Abrahamic "revealed" religions, medical advancements that allow for a longer and better life, inventions and discoveries such as electricity, radio, television, telephones, computers, the Internet and internal combustion engines, to name only a few. These allow us to communicate with each other regardless of our geographic location and to travel great distances in a relatively short period of time, thus truly making the world a much smaller place.

Yet, at the same time all these changes have taken place and continue to take place, we have not changed or adapted our spiritual/religious thinking. It has largely remained stuck in the ancient past. This can be irreversibly catastrophic in our nuclear age!

We desperately need to make real progress in our thinking about God. We need to pull our spiritual thoughts up alongside our technical and scientific advancements. One way to do this is to imagine what the world and our lives would be like if instead of just throwing our spiritual selves in reverse in order to keep them compatible with the Bible or

Koran, we also subjected all other aspects of our lives to these books. For example, we would talk to our friends and family as if the world were flat, we would suggest someone with epilepsy was not sick but simply was possessed by a demon, women who are menstruating would be separated from society for seven days in keeping with the Biblical teachings of Leviticus 15:19-30, etc. Just imagining this is enough for a sane person to get a glimpse of the total disrepair their spiritual lives are in if they are followers of these ancient nonsensical "revealed" religions and books of myth, and what real physical danger the world is in for the same reason. If we really want a world based on reason, progress and peace for ourselves and for our children, we must finally let go of teachings and traditions that promote unreasonableness and brutal violence which can only hinder progress and peace and actually put an end to Nature's purpose for us which the Designer designed into our DNA: to continue to procreate and to advance in our knowledge, wisdom and understanding.

Nuclear realities have made the waging of war an unacceptable proposition. War is very rarely justifiable; it only exposes either mankind's greed or its mental limitations at being able to formulate a rational workable solution to a problem. However, in the nuclear age our ignorance can lead to the extermination of civilization and life itself on our beautiful planet. The shallow chauvinism of the various "revealed" religions takes us all one giant step closer to that irreversible catastrophe. Deism, by its reliance on reason and rejection of non-defensive violence, serves as an unassailable block to the self-fulfilling prophecy of an apocalyptic nightmare that is so central to the major "revealed" religions.

Deism is desperately needed today. This pure and simple belief in God can, on a personal level, protect us from the manipulating egocentric clergy and their limitless ambitions for financial gain. Deism helps us realize the truth of what comedian and documentarian Bill Maher said, "Religion, to me, is a bureaucracy between man and God that I don't need." This profound realization brings with it such intense happiness and relief that it is hard to actually describe! Realizing that we don't need the bureaucracy of clergy and the volumes of pretended revelations between us and God empowers everyone who embraces it!

As the founder and director of the World Union of Deists, I frequently hear from people who've been greatly helped by Deism. One such person was a victim of a pedophile. He related how, when he was a little child, he thought God singled him out for hatred because while he was being molested he couldn't understand why it was happening to him since he was taught "Jesus loves the little children." After learning about Deism, he realized that Jesus is not God and God had nothing to do with the person who made the decision to do evil by repeatedly molesting him. Here is how he relates about how he discovered Deism: "It was while casually surfing the internet one afternoon that I happened upon a website on Deism. As I read the contents, my excitement began to grow with each paragraph. It was as if a light had switched on in my brain! This is what I had been searching for all along and I was stoked. I devoured everything I could find on Deism and the more I read, the more enlightened I became. Since that day, I have compiled a vast collection of material on Deism that I study avidly on a daily basis.

"Today, I am happy and content, knowing that I have the truth to rely on and not the destructive lies that the Bible and Christianity evoke. I love Deism."

As Deism continues to grow, it will continue to help count-less other people who are in similar dire situations as the Deist quoted above was in. Deism will also help on a global scale to pull humanity back from the brink of the Biblical self-fulfilling deadly prophesy of Armageddon. In order to accomplish these essential goals, it is of paramount importance that Deists *DO* all they can to let others know about Deism!

I believe the best way to spread Deism is to be honest and straightforward about it. There is no need or requirement to soft-pedal Deism. Compromising the truth is never right and never works in the long run. I fully embrace the mess-age Thomas Paine conveyed to Elihu Palmer in reference to Palmer's thought-provoking book *The Principles of Nature; or, A Development of the Moral Causes of Happiness and Misery Among the Human Species*. Paine wrote, "I received by Mr. Livingston the letter you wrote me, and the excellent work you have published. I see you have thought deeply on the subject, and expressed your thoughts in a strong and clear style. The hinting and inti-mating manner of writing that was formerly used on sub-jects of this kind produced skepticism, but not conviction. It is necessary to be bold." Deists must be bold in their pre-sentation of Deism to new people.

At the same time we are boldly promoting Deism, we need to do it in a nonintrusive way. For example, we should bring it up whenever the opportunity arises but stop talking about it once the person or persons we are talking to make it clear they are not interested. However, we should not stop talking about it just because someone disagrees with us. Disagreement allows for a civil free exchange of ideas, which is a requirement for progress. And just because we are, for example, pointing out absurdities in the Bible or

Koran that doesn't mean we can't do it in a very polite way. We should always be polite and avoid attacking people personally. Always remember that Deists don't hate the superstitious; we just hate the superstition!

As Deism continues to grow, we will be able to open Deist Reason Centers around the world. Deist Reason Centers will be places people can go to to learn about Deism. They will be staffed by Deists who will answer any questions people may have about Deism. They will have a library of Deism and freethought books and literature as well as videos and DVDs for people to use in order to get a better understanding of Deism and will offer free literacy classes. Each Deist Reason Center will have a quality telescope and microscope and someone knowledgeable about astronomy and the sciences who can help people study and enjoy the profoundly beautiful planets and the stars as well as the microscopic world which all point us to our Creator. I also want to have volunteer doctors, nurses, dentists and veterinarians who could help and treat people and their animals who can't afford care and/or either have no insurance or who are underinsured, and, of course, to help those who were not able to get a healing from a faith-healer!

If we are to greatly strengthen the likelihood of continuing our existence into the future, we need the natural tool of Deism to do it. When we look at extremism and what many people look at as "the lunatic fringe," we see much of it is some form of one of the "revealed" religions. From Heaven's Gate, which preached that the end was near and the only escape was suicide, to the Jewish state of Israel which teaches from the Hebrew Bible that 3,000 years ago God gave them the land the Palestinians are now living on and it is their divine right to take it from them, the lunatic fringe has largely gone without any meaningful opposition.

With Deism we finally see the arrival of that powerful opposition! Deism changes the parameters and meaning of just what defines the lunatic fringe. It changes it from rejecting widely accepted ideas to rejecting reason and Nature based ideas. For too long people have felt that if you didn't believe the prevailing thoughts and ideas of society, you were in the lunatic fringe. However, some of the strong beliefs of mainstream society were not and are not reasonable. For example, in Salem, Massachusetts in the 1600s, you would be considered a member of the lunatic fringe if you did not believe in witches and wizards. Deism sets a new standard to judge things by: Nature and reason. In the Salem example, Deists would laugh at the idea of witches and wizards because the idea of them being a reality is unnatural and unreasonable.

As we move deeper into the twenty-first century, let us recognize that it will be what we make it. Through Deism and the reason it promotes we can fashion the new century with new positive and progressive ideas and principles which will make for a much better world.

Deist Glossary

Compiled by the World Union of Deists,
taken from www.deism.com

Cult: In Deism, a cult is an embracing of unreasonable beliefs by a group of people. Based on this definition, Judaism, Christianity and Islam are all cults because their members suspend their God-given reason in order to believe or accept the unreasonable dogmatic teachings and superstitions such as God giving real estate as a gift to the Jews, the resurrection and ascension of Jesus, faith-healing and Mohammed's ascension to heaven, among many more false and unreasonable claims. Because Deism always promotes free and independent thought and reason, it is impossible for Deism to become a cult.

Deism: Deism is the recognition of an eternal universal creative force greater than that demonstrated by mankind, supported by personal observation of laws and designs in nature and the universe, perpetuated and validated by the innate ability of human reason coupled with the rejection of claims made by individuals and organized religions of having received special divine revelation.

Faith: This word has been so terribly abused by "revealed" religions that it has come to really mean the suspension of an individual's God-given reason in order to accept, or at least to tolerate, an unreasonable claim made by a "revealed" religion. It is the only way "revealed" religions can get people to accept such insane and unreasonable claims and ideas as original sin, walking on water, healing the sick without medical care, splitting the Red Sea, etc. Deists prefer to use the word "trust" instead of faith due to the twisted meaning the word "faith" has acquired after centuries of abuse from the "revealed" religions.

One key difference between Deism and the "revealed" religions is that Deists don't believe faith is required to believe in God. This quote from Voltaire sums it up, "What is faith? Is it to believe that which is evident? No. It is perfectly evident to my mind that there exists a necessary, eternal, supreme, and intelligent being. This is no matter of faith, but of reason."

God: The eternal universal creative force which is the source of the laws and designs found throughout Nature.

Intelligent Design: Intelligent Design refers to the structures in Nature, such as that of DNA, which can be observed and the complexity of which required an intelligent Designer. In this context "structure" means something arranged in a definite pattern of organization. In Deism, Intelligent Design has absolutely nothing to do with the unreasonable Biblical myth of creation.

Natural Religion: Belief in God based on the application of reason on the laws/designs of Nature as opposed to "revealed" religion which is based on alleged revelations.

Philosophy: The study of the truths and principles of being, knowledge, or conduct.

Reason: The mental powers used in forming conclusions or inferences based on facts. Deists look at reason as the second greatest gift from Nature's God to humanity, second only to life itself.

Religion: A set of beliefs concerning the cause, nature and purpose of the universe.

Revelation: The act of revealing or of making known. In the religious sense, revelation usually means divine revelation. This is meaningless, since revelation can only be revelation in the first instance. For example, if God revealed something to me, that would be a divine revelation to me. If I then told someone else what God told me, it would be mere hearsay to the person I tell. If he or she believed what I said, he or she would **not** be putting his or her trust in God, but in me, believing what I told them was actually true.

"Revealed" Religion: An organized system of belief in and worship of God (or something like God) based on the belief that God (or something like God) communicated/communicates with certain individual founders, leaders, and/or members of the particular "revealed" religion. As mentioned above, by believing in any of the "revealed" religions a believer is not putting her or his trust in God, but in the person, people or organization making the claim of receiving the divine revelation.

Trust: Trust is confidence in a person or thing based on reason and experience.

This galaxy, M51, is actually made up of two galaxies which are connected by a bridge of stars. As mentioned in Chapter Six, the coming together of two galaxies is part of the evolution of the Universe and eventually produces yet more star, planets, and life.

Frequently Asked Questions about Deism

What is the basis of Deism? Reason and nature. We see the design found throughout the known universe, and this realization brings us to a sound belief in a Designer (a.k.a. God.)

Is Deism a form of atheism? No. Atheism teaches that there is no God. Deism teaches there is a God. Deism rejects the "revelations" of the "revealed" religions but does not reject God.

If Deism teaches a belief in God, then what is the difference between Deism and the other religions like Christianity, Judaism, Islam, Buddhism, etc.? Deism is, as stated above, based on nature and reason, not "revelation." All the other religions (with the possible exception of Taoism, although superstition does play a role in both Buddhism and Taoism) make claim to special divine revelation or they have requisite "holy" books. Deism has neither. In Deism there is no need for a preacher, priest, monk or rabbi. All one needs in Deism is his or her own common sense and the creation to contemplate. Deism's lack of belief in "revelations," its lack of dogma and ritual and its lack of clergy makes Deism more of a philosophy than a religion.

Also, "revealed" religions, especially Christianity and Islam, use greed and fear to catch and hold converts. The greed is belonging to their "revealed" religion, so one can get rewards such as eternal life, and in Christianity, anything one asks for in prayer in the here and now (John 14:12-14). In combination with greed, they use fear of death. Deism does neither. Deism teaches that we should do what is right simply because it's the right thing to do. And Deism doesn't pretend we know what, if anything, happens to us after our bodies die. We love and trust God enough not to worry about it. As Thomas Paine wrote, "I consider myself in the hands of my Creator, and that He will dispose of me after this life consistently with His justice and goodness. I leave all these matter to Him, as my Creator and friend, and I hold it to be presumption in man to make an article of faith as to what the Creator will do with us hereafter."

Do Deists believe that God created the creation and the world and then just stepped back from it?   Some Deists do, and some believe God may intervene in human affairs. For example, when George Washington was faced with either a very risky evacuation of the American troops from Long Island or surrendering them, he chose the more risky evacuation. When questioned about the possibility of having them annihilated, he said it was the best he could do and the rest was up to Providence.

Do Deists pray?   Only prayers of thanks and appreciation. We don't dictate to God.

How do Deists view God?   We view God as an eternal entity whose power is equal to his/her will. The following quote from Albert Einstein also offers a good Deistic description of God: "My religion consists of a humble admiration of the illimitable superior spirit who reveals himself in the slight details we are able to perceive with our frail and feeble minds. That deeply emotional conviction of the presence of a superior reasoning power, which is revealed in the incomprehensible universe, forms my idea of God."

Is Deism a cult? It's impossible for Deism to be a cult because Deism teaches self-reliance and encourages people to constantly use their reason. Deism teaches to "question authority" no matter what the cost.

Unlike the revealed religions, Deism makes no unreasonable claims. The revealed religions encourage people to give up, or at least to suspend, their God-given reason. They like to call it faith. For example, how logical is it to believe that Moses parted the Red Sea, or that Jesus walked on water, or that Mohammed received the Koran from an angel? Suspending your reason enough to believe these tales only sets a precedent that leads to believing a Jim Jones or David Koresh.

What's Deism's answer to all the evil in the world?
Much of the evil in the world would have been overcome or removed if humanity had embraced our God-given reason from our earliest evolutionary stages. After all, all the laws of nature that we've discovered and learned to use to our advantage that make everything from computers to medicine to space travel realities, have existed eternally. But we've decided we'd rather live in superstition and fear instead of learning and gaining knowledge. It's much more soothing to believe we're not responsible for our own actions than to actually do the hard work required for success and progress. Please see Chapter Six for more details.

Deism doesn't claim to have all the answers to everything. We Deists just claim to be on the right path to those answers.

About the Author

Bob Johnson

Bob Johnson has been a Deist since 1984 and is the founder and director of the World Union of Deists. The World Union of Deists was founded on April 10, 1993 at the same time as he began the first Deistic publication since the days of Thomas Paine and Elihu Palmer, *THINK!*

In 1996 he launched the first website dedicated to Deism, www.deism.com. Currently the World Union of Deists offers three Deist webzines. *THINKonline!* is a monthly and *Bruno & Ripoll's Bulletin* which is published at least twice a month. Both of these webzines are free. To help secure the necessary funding to properly and effectively promote Deism, *Deistic Thought & Action!* is published monthly and requires a subscription. We also have a hard copy quarterly journal, *DEISM.*

The World Union of Deists strives to make Deism a household word so that people can be empowered by knowing that there is such a thing as Deism and that they have a reasonable, natural and powerful alternative to "revealed" religion, Atheism and Agnosticism in Deism.

To order additional copies of this book visit: http://www.deism.com/deismbook or send $10.00 plus $3.00 shipping to: World Union of Deists, Box 4052, Clearwater, FL 33758.

Other books offered by the World Union of Deists:

The Age of Reason, The Complete Edition by Thomas Paine

An Answer to C.S. Lewis' Mere Christianity by Bob Johnson

Principles of Nature by Elihu Palmer

Reason: The Only Oracle of Man by Ethan Allen

CPSIA information can be obtained at www.ICGtesting.com
Printed in the USA
BVOW05s0341040116

431639BV00001B/87/P